Murder Most Vile Volume Eight

18 Truly Shocking Murder Cases

Robert Keller

**Please Leave Your Review of This Book At
http://bit.ly/kellerbooks**

ISBN-13: 978-1535195690
ISBN-10: 153519569X

© 2016 by Robert Keller

robertkellerauthor.com

All rights reserved.

No part of this publication may be copied or reproduced in any format, electronic or otherwise, without the prior, written consent of the copyright holder and publisher. This book is for informational and entertainment purposes only and the author and publisher will not be held responsible for the misuse of information contain herein, whether deliberate or incidental.

Much research, from a variety of sources, has gone into the compilation of this material. To the best knowledge of the author and publisher, the material contained herein is factually correct. Neither the publisher, nor author will be held responsible for any inaccuracies.

Table of Contents

Beyond Evil 5
Hard To Kill 13
No Sex Till She's Dead 19
Rattlesnake James 27
When Love Leads To Murder 39
The Man They Couldn't Hang 45
I Don't Like Mondays 51
The Coffin Case 57
The Loss of Innocence 63
A Blueprint For Murder 69
Fit As A Fiddle And Ready To Die 75
Missing, Presumed Dead 81
In League With Satan 89
Bonfire Night 95
Dancing With The Reaper 103
The Devil In Petticoats 111
Body Parts 119
The Brighton Trunk Murders 127

Beyond Evil

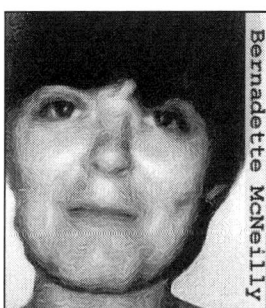
Bernadette McNeilly

In November 1993, the whole of Britain was transfixed by a murder trial, the trial of ten-year-olds Robert Thompson and Jon Venables for the murder of 4-year-old James Bulger. The boys had abducted the toddler from a Liverpool shopping mall, walked him around town for hours, then eventually taken him down to the railway tracks where they tortured and beat him to death. It was a brutal and senseless crime, perhaps one of the most horrific in the annals of British criminal history.

Just 35 miles away in nearby Manchester, another trial was underway, this one for the murder of a 16-year-old girl named Suzanne Capper. This case did not attract the same level of attention as the other, but in many ways, it involved a murder even more brutal than that of young James Bulger. Suzanne had been held captive and systematically tortured over a period of six days. She'd then been doused with gasoline and set alight. The perpetrators of this horrific act were six individuals who she had thought of as her friends.

Even at sixteen, Suzanne Capper had been through a lot in her life. Two years earlier, her mother and stepfather had divorced sending Suzanne into a period of uncertainty and instability. For most of those two years, she'd lived a shiftless existence, shuttling between her mother, her stepfather, and the local authority. She'd also begun spending time at the home of a new friend, 26-year-old mother-of-three Jean Powell.

Powell was hardly what you'd call a fitting role model for a young girl. She was a drug dealer and a fence for stolen car parts, someone who was regularly involved in violent confrontations with her neighbors. Her home at 97 Langworthy Road, Moston was a virtual turnstile for local delinquents. Most came to buy drugs or barter in stolen goods. Others, like 16-year-old Anthony Dudson, came to have sex with Powell.

Still, Suzanne appeared devoted to her new friend. She regularly babysat Powell's children for free and was always willing to help out around the house. Powell even convinced her to drop out of school and to begin working as an office cleaner in the city center. Suzanne's weekly pay packet went directly to Powell who repaid her with regular beatings.

Suzanne Capper endured all of this abuse, and never wavered in her loyalty to Jean Powell, not even when Powell took in a new lodger and the mistreatment escalated. Like Powell, Bernadette McNeilly was a young mother-of-three. She had recently rented number 91 Langworthy Road, but she and Powell had quickly become such firm friends that they had decided to move in together.

If anything, McNeilly was more dangerous than Powell. In her short time living on Langworthy Road, she'd developed a reputation for drug and booze-fueled violence. She'd threatened to burn down one neighbor's house. With another, she'd taken her threats a step further, setting their laundry alight. It wasn't long after McNeilly moved in with Powell that the violence against Suzanne Capper increased.

Matters eventually came to a head on December 7, 1992. Over the previous week, Powell and McNeilly had begun accumulating an array of petty complaints against Suzanne. The first of these related to a man named Mohammed Yussif, who Suzanne and Jean Powell had met in late November. According to the story, Powell relayed to McNeilly, Suzanne had encouraged her to have sex with Yussif and deserved "a good hiding for trying to make me go with an Arab."

Then there was the pink duffle coat that was missing from the house. Powell and McNeilly were convinced that Suzanne had taken it. Their lack of proof as to the alleged theft in no way discouraged them from plotting their revenge.

Finally, there was the most serious complaint of all. Powell and McNeilly were both promiscuous women, who routinely had sex with the succession of delinquents and drug addicts that visited the house. These included the aforementioned Anthony Dudson and Powell's ex-husband Glyn. Unsurprisingly, given this lifestyle, it wasn't long before both women were afflicted with pubic lice. The blame for this passed to Suzanne, the warped logic being that she sometimes used a downstairs bed at 97 Langworthy Road. It was enough for McNeilly to convince the others that Suzanne had to pay.

On December 7, Powell and McNeilly knocked on the door at 6 Bewley Walk, where Suzanne was staying with her stepfather. They asked Suzanne if she wanted to come over to their house. Eager to please as always, Suzanne agreed. She'd barely walked through the door at 97 Langworthy Road when Anthony Dudson and Glyn Powell grabbed her.

Dudson and Powell dragged the terrified girl into the kitchen, where they held her down and shaved off her hair and her eyebrows. After that, they made her clean up the hair from the floor, then forced her into the lounge, where Jean Powell and McNeilly were waiting. Over the hours that followed, Suzanne was subjected to a savage beating. She was punched, kicked, struck with belt buckles and a heavy wooden ornament. A cigarette was put out on her forehead; she was suffocated with a plastic bag. When she eventually collapsed, her tormentors dragged her into a small closet under the stairs, where she spent the night. The next morning her captors took her to McNeilly's home at 91 Langworthy Road. It was here that the worst of the abuse occurred.

First, Suzanne was forced to shave off her pubic hair, punishment McNeilly said, for afflicting her and Powell with pubic lice. Then she was made to lay spread-eagled on a bed and was lashed to the frame with electrical chord. With McNeilly the torturer in chief, the abuse now escalated. Suzanne was injected with amphetamines; headphones were placed over her ears and music was played at full volume for hours at a time; she was whipped and beaten, burned with cigarettes, and forced to lie in her own urine and feces.

At one point, the torturers decided that she needed to be cleaned up and poured undiluted bleach directly onto her body, then scrubbed her with hard-bristled brushes until her skin peeled off. On another, Powell's 16-year-old son, Clifford Pook, removed several of Suzanne's teeth with a pair of pliers. McNeilly, high on drugs and obviously wallowing in this inhumane cruelty, started to torment her, taking on the persona of Chucky, the evil doll from the horror movie "Child's Play." She'd start each torture session with the character's catch phrase, "Chucky's coming to play." Despite her horrific injuries and weakened state, this phrase never failed to get Suzanne screaming.

For six days and nights, Suzanne Capper endured this almost constant torment. But eventually, even her drug-addled tormentors realized that it could not go on forever. That left them with two options. They could either set her free and risk her going to the authorities, or they could kill her. To them, it must have seemed like no choice at all.

In the early hours of December 14, 1992, Suzanne was taken from the house and forced into the trunk of a stolen Fiat Panda. Glyn Powell was behind the wheel of the car, Bernice McNeilly in the passenger seat beside him. In the back were Jean Powell and her adolescent lover, Anthony Dudson. The foursome drove about 15 miles to a field outside of Stockport. There they dragged Suzanne from the car and marched her to the edge of an embankment, where McNeilly gave her a shove, sending her tumbling into a thicket of brambles. McNeilly then slid down the bank carrying a gas canister, which she emptied over Suzanne. After three failed attempts, she eventually got the gasoline to ignite. The flames quickly engulfed Suzanne and she started screaming, while McNeilly giggled and sang, "Burn baby burn!"

Eventually, Suzanne Capper's struggles subsided and she lay still on the ground, a blackened, smoldering lump, barely recognizable as human. The killers then left the scene and drove home, stopping at a liquor store to pick up some drinks on the way.

But Suzanne was not dead. With incredible courage, she clawed her ruined body up the embankment, staggered to her feet and began stumbling down the Compstall Road towards Romiley. It was 6:10 in the morning when Barry Sutcliffe and two colleagues, on their way to work, spotted her. They took her immediately to a nearby house and from there called the police and an ambulance.

Suzanne was rushed to hospital, but her injuries were horrific. Her hands and feet had been so badly burned, they looked like charcoal; on the rest of the body her flesh resembled raw meat, her face was rendered almost featureless. Still, she managed to hold on long enough to name her attackers. Then she lapsed into a coma.

Suzanne Capper died on December 18, 1992, without regaining consciousness.

All four of those involved in the killing of Suzanne Capper – Bernadette McNeilly, Jean Powell, Glyn Powell and Anthony Dudson – were arrested on December 14, within hours of Suzanne being found. In addition, Jeffrey Leigh and Clifford Pook, who had participated in torturing Suzanne, were taken into custody. At their trial, in November 1993, all were convicted.

Bernadette McNeilly and Jean Powell were both found guilty of murder and were each sentenced to life in prison with no parole for 25 years. Glyn Powell received the same sentence, while Anthony Dudson was found guilty of murder and ordered to be detained indefinitely, with a minimum of 18 years to be served. Jeffrey Leigh and Clifford Pook were found guilty of the lesser charges of false imprisonment and causing grievous bodily harm.

The final words in this horrific case belong to Suzanne's mother, Elizabeth Dunbar. "Suzanne was very forgiving," Mrs. Dunbar said. "But she was also a girl who would try to sort out her problems on her own. That's what she did in the end, she survived her ordeal long enough to name every single one of them."

Hard To Kill

They say that fact is stranger than fiction and nowhere is that more accurate than in the story of Michael Malloy, a Prohibition-era drunkard who would go on to earn the nicknames "Mike the Durable," "Iron Mike," and "the man they couldn't kill."

Born in County Donegal, Ireland, Malloy had moved to New York City in the 1920's. He'd worked for a while as a firefighter, until his habitual drinking cost him that job and he began his headlong descent towards alcoholism. By the 1930's he was taking any menial job he could get and spending all of his meager earnings in seedy speakeasies. And when the money ran out, he financed his love of rotgut whiskey on credit. It wasn't long before he'd run up tabs at all of the Bronx dives and was banned from most of them.

One bar where Malloy was still allowed to drink was a dusty little speakeasy, a single room with a bare light bulb, a few tables and a plywood bar, run by a man named Tony Marino. It wasn't that Marino was a particularly charitable man, just that Mike Malloy was deeply in hock to him and he hoped (perhaps foolishly) that Malloy would one day make good on his debt. Besides, Malloy was one of Marino's few regulars and he usually paid for his first couple of rounds with a fistful of coins. This was, of course, the era of the Great Depression. Any kind of cash flow was better than none at all.

One evening, in the winter of 1933, Marino was at his bar playing a few hands of pinochle, with four acquaintances – Joseph "Red" Murphy, Francis Pasqua, Hershey Green, and Daniel Kriesberg. The topic, as was usually the case, turned to money, or more accurately, the lack of it. Wouldn't it be great, Marino suggested, if you had a wealthy relative with one foot in the grave, preferably one who had left all of their money to you.

The men batted that idea back and forth while the night's last patron, Mike Malloy, lay snoring loudly on the sofa, sleeping off his latest bender. "On the other hand," Marino said. "If Malloy would just pay up his bar tab, I could shut down this place and retire to Florida." That raised a laugh but, when the chuckles died down, a strange silence fell over the group of men. It was as though each of them was lost in contemplation.

No one knows for sure who first raised the idea, but the crux of it was this. Mike Malloy was quite obviously drinking himself to an early grave. Just suppose that they took out a life policy on him. Suppose further, that the bar gave him an unlimited line of credit, allowing him to guzzle as much whiskey as he liked. That surely would help the process along. And hey, who got hurt in this? The conspirators made some easy money, and Malloy (who was going to die soon anyway) would be ferried to the afterlife on a river of booze. If he could choose the way he wanted to go, surely that would be it.

The first thing that needed to be done was to take out a policy on Malloy's life. That might prove a problem since none of the men was related to Malloy, but Marino had a plan. The following evening he approached Malloy with a proposal. He said that he had a brother who was critically ill. He wanted to take out an insurance policy on the brother so that his family would be provided for after he was gone. The insurance company, however, would never cover such a sick man. If Malloy would pose as his brother during a meeting with an insurance agent, Marino would be eternally grateful. Not only would he write off Malloy's tab, but he'd allow him to drink for free at the speakeasy whenever he wanted. Malloy, of course, agreed on the spot.

Thus was the plan set in motion to bring about the demise of Mike Malloy. A policy was taken out for $3,500 (around $61,000 in today's money and an absolute fortune during the Depression). Now all Marino had to do was ply Malloy with booze and wait for him to keel over. Little did Marino and his co-conspirators realize, they had chosen the worst murder victim they could possibly imagine.

At first, Marino stuck to the plan, plying Malloy with the horribly unreliable liquor of the time. This was often a toxic concoction, either due to shoddy home brewing methods or government efforts to contaminate the liquor supply. It had no contaminating effect on Malloy though. He drank himself into a stupor, passed out, slept it off and shuffled off home. The following day he'd be back for more. Marino then tried adding antifreeze to the booze, then turpentine, then horse liniment. Finally, he resorted to rat poison. The old soak guzzled it all down and appeared none the worse for it.

With the liquor having failed to do its job, the conspirators next tried to poison Malloy with contaminated food. First, they fed him raw oysters that had been marinated in wood alcohol. Then they gave him a plate of rotten sardine sandwiches, further contaminated with metal shavings and crushed glass. Durable Mike woofed it all down with relish. He even asked for seconds.

A month passed, during which the conspirators began to grow increasingly impatient for their windfall. Each evening they sat at the bar with eyes cast anxiously towards the door, praying that Malloy wouldn't show up. Each night he staggered in, greeted everyone jovially and got down to the serious work of drinking himself into a stupor.

New methods were called for and the conspirators hit on a plan one frigid February night. After Malloy passed out they carried him to a nearby park, laid him down in the snow, ripped open his coat and shirt and for good measure poured a few buckets of water over him. He was back at the bar the next evening without so much as a sniffle. Next, they hired a taxi driver to run Malloy over as he crossed the street. The result was a broken collarbone and a couple of days in the hospital. Malloy was soon back on his familiar perch at the bar.

But now the conspirators decided that enough was enough. The next attempt had to be their last, the method they chose foolproof. One of them suggested gas. This time, after Malloy passed out, the men carried him to an empty apartment in a nearby building, ran a hose from the gas line to Malloy's mouth and turned on the valve. 'Iron Mike' Malloy lasted just minutes before succumbing to the lethal carbon monoxide gas.

After his death, Malloy's 'friends' at the speakeasy generously clubbed together to pay for a burial, performed by Frank Pasqua, who ran a funeral home. Earlier, they'd bribed a doctor to record Malloy's cause of death as alcohol poisoning. Now, at last, they were free to collect their ill-gotten gains.

Unfortunately for the conspirators, booze and secrets are poor bedfellows. Under the influence, one of their number told someone the story of the indestructible Mike Malloy. That person told someone else and before you knew it, every speakeasy in the Bronx was abuzz with the incredible tale. It was only a matter of time before the story reached the police.

By the time Malloy's body was exhumed, Marino and his cohorts were probably wishing that they'd had him cremated. But it was too late for that now. An autopsy proved that Malloy had died of carbon monoxide poisoning and members of the so-called 'Murder Trust' were quickly rounded up.

Of the five, only Hershey Green escaped the executioner. Tony Marino, Joseph Murphy, Francis Pasqua and Daniel Kriesberg all went to the electric chair in the summer of 1934.

No Sex Till She's Dead

It started as a joke, a text message between teenaged lovers complete with the obligatory "LOL" at the end. But as time went by and hundreds more texts passed between Melissa Todorovic and David Bagshaw, the jest hardened into something far more serious, the fantasy morphed into a plan. Melissa wanted David's ex-girlfriend, Stefanie Rengel, dead. And she was prepared to withhold sex from her lover until he killed her.

Bagshaw and Todorovic first met while they were both attending East York Collegiate in Toronto. He was a high school football star with a learning disability, she a bookish straight-A student, complete with glasses, and braces on her teeth. Highly insecure about her looks, 15-year-old Melissa was astounded that someone like David would be interested in her. She quickly became obsessively jealous over him, a behavior she'd also exhibited in several earlier relationships.

For his part, David was a far from ideal boyfriend. He often cheated on Melissa, and on occasion, he beat her. Yet Melissa refused to consider ending the relationship. When her mother urged her to break up with David, she responded, "Who's going to look at somebody with braces and glasses when there's so many pretty girls in high school?"

Melissa's initial fixation with David's ex, started over an innocent remark, probably intended to make her jealous. After David commented that he still thought Stefanie was pretty, Melissa began obsessively visiting Stefanie's Facebook page to look at pictures of her. Then, after word got back to Melissa that David had been flirting with Stefanie, and with other girls, she was furious.

On May 22, 2007, in an on-line chat session with David, she threatened, "I'm going to fucking stab her if I want to. Then I'll just kill her." The following day, David sent her a text offering to bring her a knife. "I've already got one," Melissa sent back. "I even brought it to school today LOL."

And so it began, one flippant remark that grew into an extended conversation – over a hundred texts – about the murder of an innocent teenager. Melissa wondered if she could convince her brother to rape Stefanie. Then she urged David to kidnap Stefanie and take her to a place where Melissa could kill her. When he demurred, she shot back, "Fine, no sex until then."

As the summer continued, the texts passing between Melissa and David became increasingly graphic. At one point, Melissa fantasized about cutting off Stephanie's breasts, slicing her open and throwing her from a high building. Then, these wild imaginings started to become something even scarier, an actual plan for murder. Melissa began insisting that David should be the one to do the killing. "I don't want to kill her, LOL," she wrote. "Like I don't care if someone kills her, but I don't want to. LOL." By the fall of 2007, after much haranguing by his girlfriend, David appeared to be falling in line.

On the night of October 20, David walked to Stefanie's home and phoned her from the driveway, asking her to meet him outside. He was carrying a knife with him but once Stefanie appeared, he decided that he could not go through with it. Instead, he offered a bizarre warning to the bemused Stefanie. "Melissa wants me to stab you," he said. "When she calls, tell her I tried so she'll stop pestering me to kill you."

The incident badly frightened Stefanie, and she immediately told her mother (a Toronto police officer) about it. Stefanie's mother, Patricia Hung, then phoned Melissa and David's parents. However, she made a tragic mistake in underestimating the seriousness of the threat and stopped short of pressing criminal charges.

Melissa and David, meanwhile, appeared undeterred by parental warnings. They continued texting back and forth, now suggesting that they should get a gun and shoot Stefanie. "I want her dead, David. LOL," Melissa wrote. "We've been through this. Even if it takes you a week."

By now, the dynamic in Melissa and David's relationship had shifted and there can be little doubt that she was the one calling the shots. On December 17, she sent him a text threatening to go out with other boys unless he followed through. "Ur getting blocked until u kill her," she wrote. Then she continued nagging and threatening, leading to David again ending up outside Stefanie's house, this time on New Year's Eve. A couple of calls were made to Stefanie's phone, but if she got them she did not respond. Eventually, David walked away, having again failed in his mission.

Melissa was furious at David's failure. In revenge, she cut him off. He, in desperation, sent her a series of increasingly anxious texts "Where r u?" "Ur cheating," and "Why won't you answer me?" Eventually, at around 3 p.m. on January 1, Melissa called back, but it was only to remind him of her threat to sleep with another boy unless he killed Stefanie. A few dozen texts later and David called Melissa to tell her that he was on his way to Stefanie's house. It was 5:50 p.m. and Stefanie was at home alone with her brother, Ian.

At 6:08 Stefanie Rengel's cell phone rang. The caller did not identify himself and the line was bad but Stefanie was certain that it was Steve Lopez, an ex-boyfriend, on the other end. He said that he was standing outside and needed to talk to her. He sounded upset. Not even bothering to pull on a coat, Stefanie dashed out of the door. She told Ian that she'd be right back. It was a promise she'd never get to keep.

David Bagshaw was hiding in the bushes holding an eight-inch kitchen knife. At five-foot-11 and 240-pounds, he towered over Stefanie as he broke cover and stepped into her path. She'd barely had time to react when he thrust the blade forward and ripped through her sweater and into her flesh. The first blow was delivered with such ferocity that the knife sliced through her chest cavity and clattered against her spine. Another lacerated her lung and penetrated her liver; a third caused the contents of her stomach to seep into the peritoneal cavity. Six stab wounds were inflicted in total, before the killer fled the scene. Then Stefanie staggered across the road, clutching the jagged stomach wound while dark blood seeped between her fingers and stained the pristine snow.

Gavin Shoebottom, a 34-year-old accountant, was driving past when he spotted the obviously injured teen. He slammed on the brakes and jumped from his vehicle to offer assistance. Stefanie moaned in pain as he reached her. "Hold your stomach," he told her as he dialed 911. Then he ran back to his car to fetch a bed sheet, which he held to the wounds in an attempt to stem the bleeding. "Who did this to you?" he asked Stefanie.

"He went that way," she mumbled, wincing through the pain.

"Who was it?"

"David Bagshaw."

By the time the paramedics arrived, Stefanie had slipped into unconsciousness. By the time they got her to Toronto East General, she was beyond help. Stefanie Rendel, the 14-year-old who had done nothing wrong other than to become the subject of another teenager's obsession, was dead.

But at least the police had the name of her killer. After stabbing Stefanie, David Bagshaw had fled to a friend's house, discarding the knife and his bloody jacket on the way. He'd then called Melissa to tell her that the deed was done. She'd told him to stay where he was until she phoned him. She had then waited 15 minutes before calling Stefanie's phone. Getting no reply, she had decided that perhaps David had come through after all. She'd then phoned him back and told him to take a taxi to her house. Once there, she'd give him his reward, but only after he'd described the murder to her in great detail.

The first that Stefanie's mother and stepfather heard of the murder was when their son Ian phoned them to say that there'd been a stabbing in the neighborhood. Patricia and James were visiting family at the time but they immediately left for home. They arrived to find their road clogged with police vehicles, yellow crime scene tape strung around a clump of bushes, blood in the snow. They didn't know yet who the victim was but they'd tried phoning Stefanie on the way home and had got no reply. After speaking to officers at the scene, the Hungs learned that the victim had been taken to Toronto East General. It was only after arrival at the hospital that they learned the dreadful truth. Their 14-year-old daughter was dead. Savagely slain for a reason no one could yet comprehend.

By now, of course, a concerted police operation was underway to find David Bagshaw. As part of that effort, lead investigator, Detective Sergeant Steve Ryan, rounded up several of Bagshaw's friends for questioning. One of those brought in was Melissa Todorovic's and it wasn't long before she dropped a bombshell, admitting that it was she who had urged David to kill Stefanie.

Ryan then immediately ended the interview and placed her under arrest.

Melissa Todorovic and David Bagshaw were tried separately for the murder of Stefanie Rengel. While he was teary-eyed and weepy at his trial, Melissa showed little remorse. She sat rigidly throughout, an entirely blank expression on her face, displaying no emotion even when she read a prepared statement, apologizing to Stefanie's family. Psychiatrists who examined her concluded that she was suffering from a borderline personality disorder.

But that held little sway with the nine men and three women on the jury. After deliberating for twenty hours, they found Melissa Todorovic guilty of first-degree murder. Judge Ian Nordheimer then accepted the prosecution's application to have her sentenced as an adult. He sentenced her to life imprisonment, rather than the maximum six years she would have received as a juvenile.

David Bagshaw, who was 17 years old at the time of the murder and therefore still a juvenile, was also treated as an adult offender and sentenced to life in prison.

Rattlesnake James

Anyway you cut it, Mary Busch was an attractive woman. The tall, statuesque blond was looking for work as a manicurist and when she responded to an ad for just such a vacancy at a Los Angeles barbershop in 1935, the owner of the establishment, Robert James, was instantly smitten. He hired her on the spot, then set about seducing her. Within weeks, the couple was married. Three months later, 27-year-old Mary was pregnant with their first child.

But there were a few things that Mary didn't know about her new husband. She didn't know, for example, that Robert had been married four times before and had yet to divorce his most recent wife. She didn't know that at least one of his former wives had perished in highly questionable circumstances. She didn't know that another of Robert's relatives, a nephew, had also died a suspicious death, or that Robert had benefitted from an insurance policy taken out on his life. There was no way, of course, that she could have known these things. To her, the handsome Robert James was the perfect husband, a well-to-do entrepreneur who was also a gentleman.

Indicative of that latter quality was Robert's reaction when his wife complained of feeling ill at the barbershop on the evening of August 3, 1935. The ever attentive husband, he immediately summoned a taxi and sent his wife home, dispatching her with instructions to take a tonic and then go directly to bed to rest up. Even after Mary departed he appeared distracted, concerned for her wellbeing. Before leaving that night, he handed his keys to one of his employees, instructing the man to open the shop the next day, as he would not be in. Then he left to attend to his ailing wife.

When he returned to work on Monday, August 5, James still appeared preoccupied. He told his employees that Mary was still not at her best but might be in later in the day. By closing time, however, she had still not put in an appearance. James had, in the interim, invited two of Mary's friends - Viola Lueck and her boyfriend Jim Pemberton – to join him and Mary for dinner at their home. At closing time (around 7:30) the couple met him at his shop and the three of them traveled together to the James' home, a comfortable pink stucco in La Canada, a suburb of Los Angeles.

Arriving at the home, James and his guests were surprised to find the place in darkness. That surprise was elevated to alarm when a search found no sign of Mary in the house. James then suggested looking in the garden. Mary likes sitting by the pond watching the goldfish, he said. Sure enough, Mary was where he'd suggested she might be. Except that she was face down in the water, her arms and legs splayed out behind her.

The police and a doctor were soon on the scene, where Mary was pronounced dead in an apparent drowning. James had a ready theory for investigators as to what might have happened. Mary, he said, had suffered dizzy spells throughout her pregnancy. He suggested that she must have come out to look at the fish, suffered a spell and collapsed into the pond, striking her head on a rock on the way down. It was a viable hypothesis, except that there was no indication of a head injury. There was, however, a pronounced swelling and discoloration to the right leg, as well as a nasty gash to the right big toe.

The doctor was uncertain as to what might have caused these injuries but the police found a possible explanation when they searched the house and found a note, written in Mary's hand, and addressed to her sister. In it, she said that she was feeling ill and had pain in her leg. Something had bitten her while she'd been watering the garden earlier in the day and the injury was making her feel nauseous and dizzy. The police were initially suspicious of this fortuitous find, but just as they were about to haul James down to the station for further questioning, a witness appeared who seemed to back up his version of events. James' neighbor, a retired military man named Dinsley, said that he'd seen Mary wandering alone near the pool that evening.

The origin of the mysterious injuries on Mary's leg soon also had an explanation - she'd been bitten by a rattlesnake. Was it possible that the snake had struck while she was in the garden, causing her to plunge into the water and drown? It seemed so. At any rate, the death appeared accidental and that was how the coroner's inquest ruled it.

Robert James wasted little time mourning his dead wife and unborn child. As soon as the verdict was in, he filed a claim on his wife's recently acquired insurance policies. There were two of these, one with the Mutual Life Insurance Company and the other with Occidental Life Insurance. The total sum insured was $10,000, a considerable sum in those days. James, however, wanted $21,400, citing a double indemnity clause. The insurers refused and the matter headed to court.

Had Robert James accepted the $10,000 payout on offer, he would likely have gotten away scot-free. The court proceedings however, saw an insurance investigator assigned to the case and it wasn't long before he picked up some very interesting information about James. For starters, it turned out that James had not been legally married to Mary Busch as he'd not yet bothered to divorce his former wife. That alone might have negated his claim, but the insurers offered to settle at $3,500 and James was reluctantly forced to accept.

But that was not all the investigator found out about Robert James. James, in fact, was not even his real name. He was Major Raymond Lisemba, born to poor sharecropping folk in Alabama in 1895. James would likely have been destined for the same miserable existence had not his sister and brother-in-law intervened on his behalf. They paid for him to attend barbering school, thus providing him with a trade by which to earn his living.

James married for the first time in 1921 when he was 26 years old. The marriage, however, was short-lived. His bride, Maud Duncan, soon divorced him, citing sadistic cruelty and his perverse sexual tastes.

Unperturbed, James moved to Kansas, where he opened a barbershop and married again. Things were going well until an angry father arrived at James' place of business wielding a shotgun and accusing James of impregnating his young daughter. Rather than face up to his responsibilities, James skipped town, abandoning his wife. He turned up next in Fargo, North Dakota, where he bought another barbershop. In 1932, he married a woman named Winona Wallace, immediately taking out an insurance policy on her life.

Three months later, James took his new bride to Pike's Peak for a belated honeymoon. Shortly after they arrived, the couple was involved in an auto accident during which Mrs. James suffered a serious head injury while James walked away from the wreck with nary a scratch. Investigators arriving on the scene noticed a bloody hammer on the back seat, but paid no attention to it, nor to the fact that despite claiming that he'd jumped from the speeding vehicle, James' suit was impeccable, with neither a scuff nor a speck of dust.

If James' intention had been to kill his wife, however, he'd failed. Despite her horrific injuries, Winona recovered after spending two weeks in the hospital. Police questioned her about the accident but the head trauma she'd suffered had deprived her of any memory of the event. James, meanwhile, decided that his wife's recovery would be aided by a period of quiet rest. To this extent, he took her to a remote cabin in Manitou Springs, Colorado.

On the evening of October 14, 1932, James hiked from the cabin to the local grocery store to pick up some supplies. He asked clerk Gerald Rogers to deliver his purchases then decided to hitch a ride with Rogers. When the two men arrived at James' cabin he told Rogers to bring the groceries to the kitchen while he went looking for his wife, Winona. Moments later, James returned to the kitchen. He appeared to be in a state of shock. Asking Rogers to follow him, he walked down the short passage to the bathroom. Winona James lay on her back in a tub of soapy water. She appeared to have drowned.

When the police arrived James was ready with his theory of how his wife may have died. He suggested that Winona had not yet fully recovered from the car accident and that the hot water of the tub had likely caused her to become dizzy and slip below the surface. He, in fact, pressed the medical examiner to state this in his report but backed off when the M.E. told him that he would have to conduct and autopsy to verify James' hypothesis.

James' motive in attempting to link the death to the car accident was obvious. He was hoping to trigger the double indemnity clause. Even without it, he pocketed over $14,000 from the life insurance policies he had taken out on Winona immediately after their wedding. He bought a new car with the proceeds, a top of the range, Pierce-Arrow convertible. Then he headed back to Alabama where he remarried within months.

But if James was hoping to run his deadly scam with his new bride (and there is strong evidence to suggest that he was) he came up short. The savvy woman declined his generous offer to insure her life and refused to sign the paperwork. "People you insure always die of something strange," she said. A short while later, she walked out on him.

It was a setback, but not one that was about to deter someone as determined as Robert James. When his nephew, Cornelius Wright, arrived in town on leave from the Navy, James took the young serviceman under his wing. He insisted that Cornelius use his swanky sports sedan to get around town, an offer the young man gratefully accepted. Unfortunately, the arrangement ended in tragedy. Cornelius was driving along a cliffside road when he lost control of the vehicle and plunged over the edge. James, fortuitously, had insured his nephew's life and received a large payout from the insurance company.

The Wright family had been good to Robert James, paying for him to attend barbering school and thus saving him from the backbreaking life of a sharecropper. But they had barely recovered from the death of their son, when James plunged them into a new crisis, seducing their 18-year-old daughter, Lois. Lois was, of course, James' niece, but when her parents sought to intervene, James persuaded her to run away with him to Los Angeles. There, he set her up in an apartment while he went in search of his next meal ticket. Mary Busch was the unfortunate victim selected for that role.

The insurance investigator who had uncovered the sordid details of Robert James' past felt there was enough evidence of wrongdoing to involve the police. He handed over his files to the LAPD. They, in turn, set up surveillance on James and bugged his home. They were hoping that he might say something that would connect him to the death of Mary Busch, but the wily James said nothing to implicate himself. However, James had always been a ladies man and it was this that would lead to his eventual downfall. After Mary's death, he took up again with his niece Lois, leading on April 19, 1936, to his arrest for incest, a felony under California law. Convicted on that charge, he was sentenced to 50 years in prison. And his troubles had only just begun.

The James' incest trial received considerable newspaper coverage, resulting in a number of tip-offs. One of those led detectives to a short order cook from Hermosa Beach named Charles Hope. Hope, according to the tipster, had told him a bizarre story about the death of Mary Busch.

Brought in for questioning, Hope initially denied knowing anything about Mary's death. It was only when investigators suggested that he might find himself at the end of a rope that he eventually cracked and related the gruesome details of Mary's murder.

According to Hope, he first met Robert James when he stopped at his barbershop for a haircut. Down on his luck, Hope had asked James if he could have the haircut on credit as he had a job interview. James eventually relented, but he wanted a strange favor in return. He wanted Hope to acquire two rattlesnakes for him. When Hope initially refused, James sweetened the deal by offering him $100 if he helped him obtain the serpents. Desperate for money, Hope agreed.

A few days later, Hope bought three rattlers from a sideshow in Long Beach. The snakes, however, appeared lethargic and not aggressive enough for James' liking. A subsequent pair also did not meet with the barber's approval. Finally, Hope traveled to Pasadena where he bought a couple of Colorado diamond-backs from a dealer named Snake Joe Houtenbrink. These snakes, named Lethal and Lightning, were tried out on some chickens and definitely lived up to their names.

James meanwhile, had been working on Mary, pestering her to end her pregnancy. When Mary said no, James informed her that he did not want children and would have to divorce her if she refused to have an abortion. Eventually, he bullied her into it.

The date was set for August 4, 1935. On that night, James plied a tearful Mary with liquor, then convinced her that she'd have to be tied down to the kitchen table during the procedure. He also told her that the doctor insisted on her being blindfolded so that she would not be able to identify him. With the blindfold in place, James added a gag for good measure.

With the gullible Mary now entirely under his control, James moved on to the next part of his diabolical plan. He ordered Hope to bring the box holding the snakes into the kitchen. Then he slid back the lid and forced Mary's foot into the box. The snakes attacked immediately, sinking their fangs into the helpless woman's flesh three times.

Satisfied that the rattlers had injected enough venom to kill his wife, James withdrew her foot from the box. He then instructed Hope to get rid of the snakes and the box and to return when he was done. He warned Hope not to get any ideas about going to the police as he was an accessory to the crime and equally responsible. Hope did not need much convincing. After releasing the snakes in an arroyo, he returned to the James' residence where he and Robert James sat drinking whiskey in the garage while they waited for Mary to die.

But by 1:30 in the morning Mary was still very much alive, although she was clearly in agony, her leg swollen and turning a deep shade of purple. Frustrated, James decided to move things along. After cutting Mary loose, he carried her limp body to the bathroom and drowned her in the tub. He and Hope then dumped the corpse in the fishpond to make it appear that she'd accidentally fallen in and drowned.

The story Hope told, horrified even the hardened detectives who had listened to his confession. Yet, given what they now knew about Robert James, it also seemed entirely plausible. James predictably denied every last syllable and tried to pin the murder on Hope. But where was the motive, detectives wanted to know? Why would Hope have cooked up such an elaborate scheme to murder a woman he didn't even know? To that, Robert James could offer no answer.

The trial of Robert James and Charles Hope lasted five weeks and ended with a guilty verdict for both men. Hope, who had agreed to turn State's evidence, was sentenced to life in prison. James was sentenced to death by hanging.

But Robert James was not about to go easily. Over the next six years (an inordinately long time for that era), he worked the appeals system. Eventually, however, his time ran out.

Robert "Rattlesnake" James kept his date with the hangman on May 9, 1942. The state of California had, in the interim, changed its method of execution to the gas chamber but James would still be executed by hanging, the last condemned man to die by that method in California. In an additional twist, the rope was measured too short, meaning that James did not die by the instant snap of his neck as he was supposed to. Instead, he choked to death, lingering at the end of the rope for ten minutes before his struggles ceased.

When Love Leads To Murder

Mariette Bosch

The Bosch family – Justin, his wife Mariette, and their three children – had moved to Botswana to escape the epidemic of violent crime in their home country, South Africa. That was in 1992, and Botswana, a former British colony, was booming. The Boschs bought a house in Phakalane, a wealthy enclave in the capital, Gaborone, popular with ex-pat South Africans. They were able to afford a maid and a full-time gardener. Stay-at-home-mom Mariette spent her days shopping and visiting friends. On the weekends, she and Justin frequented the city's casinos and golf courses. Several upmarket game lodges were just a short drive away and the Bosch family visited them often. Life was good.

But then in 1995, tragedy struck. Justin was killed in a car accident. Mariette, devastated and without the support of her extended family, was comforted by Tienie and Ria Wolmarans, fellow South Africans who she and Justin had befriended in Botswana. Pretty soon, the threesome was inseparable. Mariette became a near permanent fixture in the Wolmarans household. She and Ria became firm friends. They baked together, shared the school run and went on shopping junkets. They took pottery classes and played bridge with friends. When Ria and Tienie took their children on a family vacation, they insisted that Mariette and her brood join them.

But all was not as picture perfect as it seemed. There were problems in the Wolmarans marriage, problems that were exacerbated by Mariette's constant presence. At 45, the tall blond was still an attractive woman. Within five months of Justin's death, she and Tienie were involved in a passionate affair, an affair that quickly deepened into something more serious. Tienie began talking about leaving his wife. Soon, Mariette began to pressure him into making good on his promise. When he failed to do so, she decided to take matters into her own hands.

On the night of June 26, 1996, Ria Wolmarans was home alone. Tienie was working away at the time, and the couple's daughter, Maryna, was out visiting friends. Sometime during the evening, Ria went to the kitchen to prepare a snack and a cup of tea. She was walking back to the living room carrying a tray when she encountered a gun-wielding intruder. Two shots were fired, striking Ria in the chest and stomach. She died where she fell and was found later that evening by her daughter.

The tragic, and apparently motiveless, killing baffled the Gaborone police. On the surface, it looked like a burglary gone wrong. But that was unusual in a low-crime country like Botswana. Burglars here simply did not carry guns, let alone use them against helpless victims.

Tienie Wolmarans, meanwhile, appeared to be taking his wife's death in his stride. A month after Ria's death, he and Mariette moved in together. Two months later, they secretly became engaged and visited South Africa to shop for a wedding dress.

Then, out of the blue, there was a break in the case. In early October 1996, Judith Bosch, Mariette's sister-in-law, walked into a police station in Pietersburg, South Africa. She was carrying a Browning 9 mm pistol and she had a story to tell. According to Judith, this was the weapon that had killed Ria Wolmarans. It had been handed to her husband for safekeeping. By whom, the police wanted to know? By Mariette Bosch, Judith said.

Judith then went on to add detail to her story. She said that as far back as June 1996, Mariette had confessed to her that she was in love with Tienie. In early June, Mariette had borrowed a 9mm Browning pistol from a friend in South Africa, claiming that she wanted to do some target shooting. Later that month, she'd given the weapon to her brother (Judith's husband), asking him to keep it in a "safe place." When she'd first heard about the shooting, Judith had wondered whether Mariette might be involved. After much soul searching, she'd eventually decided to go to the police.

To a police force that had already decided that the murder was the result of a botched burglary, the story seemed tenuous, at best. Nonetheless, they had an obligation to at least test fire the weapon. To their surprise, they got a ballistic match. This was indeed the weapon that had killed Ria Wolmarans. That made it likely that either Tienie or Mariette had pulled the trigger. On October 7, 1996, both were brought in for questioning. Tienie was later released after it was determined that he was nowhere near Gaborone on the night of the murder.

Mariette, however, had no such alibi. She would remain in custody for ten months, refusing to speak to police. When she eventually broke her silence, she admitted to bringing the gun into Botswana but named Hennie Coetzee, Ria's former boss, as her killer.

The murder trial of Mariette Bosch eventually got underway at Botswana's Lobatse High Court in December 1999. In the interim, the accused murderess had been out on bail and had used her period of freedom to marry her lover, Tienie Wolmarans.

As is commonplace in Botswana, there was no jury. The evidence would be weighed by a judge, who would decide both the verdict and the sentence. Right from the outset, things began to go wrong for Mariette Bosch. The defense's contention that Hennie Coetzee had hypnotized her by slipping a drug into her drink, and had then instructed her to bring in a gun from South Africa for him, was quite frankly bizarre. The prosecution presented a far more likely scenario. Mariette had become frustrated by Tienie's continued wavering and had decided to take action. After obtaining the murder weapon from her friend in South Africa, she'd called on the Wolmarans home on June 26, knowing Ria would be alone. Using a house key that Ria had generously provided her, she'd entered the home, found Ria in the passageway, and shot her to death.

This theory was backed up by ballistics, and by several witnesses. The prosecution's star turn, in fact, was Judith Bosch, a woman who appeared to have little love for her sister-in-law. Her testimony about the affair and the murder weapon would be the cornerstone of the prosecution case. When Mariette's alibi, that she hadn't left her home on the night of the murder, was rebuffed by the testimony of her maid, there could be only one outcome. On February 21, 2000, Justice Isaac Aboagye found Mariette Bosch guilty of pre-meditated murder. He then donned the black cap and sentenced her to death by hanging.

The sentence was treated with shock in the media in both Botswana and South Africa. Botswana, after all, had not executed a woman in over three decades. Still, few believed that Bosch would be put to death. There was still the appeals process to go through. General consensus was that the sentence would be reduced to a term of imprisonment, if not overturned entirely.

The Botswana Appeals Court is a unique body, comprising judges from the United Kingdom, South Africa, Zimbabwe and Nigeria. The court sits twice a year in January and July and it was in January 2001 that Mariette Bosch's case came before it. By then, Mariette had spent a year in solitary confinement and it had taken its toll. The once vivacious blonde looked gaunt and haggard, much older than her years. Her usual, immaculately applied, makeup was absent and her hair was drawn into a tight ponytail. Despite what she had done, it was easy to feel a twinge of pity.

The court, however, was disinclined to be merciful. Describing Bosch as a "wicked and despicable woman," acting Judge President Timothy Aguda, announced his ruling. The appeal was dismissed. Mariette Bosch was going to the gallows. Mariette seemed shell shocked at the outcome. Tienie Wolmarans and Mariette's three children broke down and cried.

She had once been a well-off, upper-middle-class woman who took great care over her appearance and wore only the finest couture. But Mariette Bosch spent her final days in a tiny cell, wearing a rough, brown prison dress and subsisting on a diet of tripe and morogo (a kind of African wild spinach). For ablutions, she had a bucket, to sleep, a hard mattress.

On the last day of her life, Saturday, March 31, 2001, she was woken early, for the execution that was to take place at 6:00 a.m. She was not allowed any last minute visits by family, nor was she offered any special last meal. No outside witnesses were present at the execution. Indeed, there was no advance warning of it at all. Not even Mariette's family was informed.

When Tienie Wolmarans and Mariette's daughters arrived at the prison that Saturday hoping to visit, they were informed that Mariette had been put to death and buried in the prison grounds. They were then handed her personal belongings and ordered to leave.

The execution of Mariette Bosch provoked an outcry from international human rights groups. The government of Botswana however, was adamant that she had received a fair trial and had been put to death humanely, in accordance with the country's laws. A government spokesman also reminded the media that there was another party to be considered, the murdered woman, Ria Wolmarans.

The Man They Couldn't Hang

One of the biggest arguments against the death penalty is that the judicial system is fallible. Mistakes happen and there have been several well-documented cases of innocent men being executed, like Timothy Evans in the UK, or Jesse Tafero in the United States. Recent studies, in fact, suggest that at least 4% of death row prisoners in the United States are innocent of the crimes for which they were convicted. And in recent years several convictions have been overturned, thanks to advances in forensic technology.

At the time that John Lee was convicted of the murder of his employer, however, forensic science was in its infancy. There was no fingerprinting, no DNA, no Innocence Project to take up the case of a wrongly convicted person. Lee was convicted on the flimsiest of evidence and sentenced to hang. It appeared nothing could save him. Amazingly, something did.

John Henry George Lee was born in the Devon village of Abbotskerswell on August 15, 1864. As a young man, he served in the Royal Navy aboard the training ship HMS Implacable. However, he was of a somewhat light-fingered persuasion and in 1883, he was convicted of theft and sentenced to a prison term with hard labor at Exeter prison.

Upon his release, the 19-year-old Lee sought new employment and was hired as a footman by an elderly spinster named Emma Ann Whitehead Keyse. Miss Keyse, who had been a maid of honor to Queen Victoria, lived in beautiful Babbacombe Bay, South Devon. She was well off (but not wealthy), religious by nature and forthright in her opinions. She already employed Lee's half-sister, Elizabeth Harris, as a cook and it was through this family connection that Lee obtained his position. Lee, however, was not suited to a life in service. He was a cocky young man, inherently dishonest and with an aversion to hard work. It wasn't long before Miss Keyse let it be known that she was dissatisfied with his performance. She even reduced his wages and threatened to fire him if he failed to address his shortcomings. Lee, bluff as always, is said to have taken these threats in his stride.

On the morning of November 15, 1884, one of Miss Keyse's servants woke to the smell of something burning. Rising from her bed, the woman went to investigate its source, her search leading her eventually to the pantry. There a horrific scene awaited her, her employer lying on the ground, doused in fuel oil, her throat crudely hacked, burning newspaper surrounding her. The servant quickly doused the flames then checked on her mistress. Realizing that Miss Keyse was beyond help, she ran back to the servants' quarters and raised the alarm.

The village police were quickly on the scene and just as quickly they honed in on John Lee as the killer. On what evidence, you might ask? On the condition of the corpse, for one thing. Miss Keyse's throat had been so viciously slashed that she was almost decapitated. It seemed incomprehensible to the police that a woman could have inflicted such a wound, and as Lee was the only man in the household it had to be him. Then there was a cut on Lee's arm. He claimed he'd received it while forcing a window. He even pointed out the broken glass. The police did not believe him. Then there was motive. Everyone in the household knew that Miss Keyse had reprimanded Lee for poor performance, docked his pay and threatened to fire him.

John Lee was charged with murder and escorted to Exeter Gaol to await his trial. It looked like an open and shut case and so it proved. Despite his protestations of innocence, Lee was found guilty and sentenced to hang. His execution date was set for February 23, 1885.

The story of the horrific murder was extensively covered in the press, both in Britain and abroad. And nowhere was there much public sympathy for John Lee. On the day of his execution, a drab, drizzly Monday, a large crowd gathered in front of Exeter Gaol, eagerly waiting for news of his demise. Inside, Lee was roused from his cell and with arms pinioned was flanked by two guards on the short walk to the gallows. A priest walked close behind, reciting a prayer as Lee climbed the steps to the scaffold. There, the hangman, James Berry, placed a hood over Lee's head and positioned him with his feet on the trapdoor. He fixed the noose in place then grasped the lever and pulled it back … nothing. The trapdoor didn't budge.

Berry gave the lever another tug, then pushed it back and forth. The trapdoor refused to open. On Berry's instruction, the guards moved Lee aside and stomped down on the trap with their heavy boots. It remained stubbornly in place. Berry then called for a carpenter and instructed him to shave away the edges of the trapdoor. A heavy weight was placed on top of it and Berry pushed the lever. This time, the trapdoor snapped open right away.

Confident that the technical hitch had now been resolved, Berry got Lee back into position. The priest started up his prayer again. Berry reached for the lever and pushed. The trapdoor refused to budge.

Frustrated now, Berry ordered that Lee be returned to his cell. He then called in a team of workmen who spent twenty minutes applying a plane to the edges of the trapdoor, then oiling its hinges and finally testing the apparatus. Three trials were carried out and each time the trap opened perfectly. Yet the minute John Lee stepped onto the scaffold again, the contraption developed a malfunction.

Time and again Berry leaned on the lever, time and again it failed him. Lee was again escorted back to his cell, while word of the botched execution was relayed to the Home Secretary, Sir William Vernon Harcourt. Within hours, Harcourt sent word commuting Lee's sentence to life in prison.

John Lee would spend a total of twenty-two years behind bars, during which time he remained steadfast in his pleas of innocence. He petitioned a succession of Home Secretaries for a reprieve until

1907, when one was finally granted to him. Freed from the Portland Jail, he billed himself as John 'Babbacombe' Lee and started touring the country, telling a hugely romanticized and wildly inaccurate version of his life story. Despite the years that had passed, people were still fascinated by the tale of 'The Man They Couldn't Hang' and Lee drew huge crowds wherever he appeared. There was even a silent film made about his life.

After years locked up in prison, Lee gleefully exploited his notoriety, playing on the public's belief that God had intervened on his behalf because he had been wrongfully convicted. Women were attracted to him and he married one of them, a nurse named Jessie Augusta Bulled in January 1909. He would father two children by Jessie although by the time the second was born he had absconded with a barmaid, leaving his wife and children destitute.

Not much is known about Lee after that date. The last reported sighting of him was in Brighton, circa 1916. Various reports place him in America, Canada, and Australia after that date, although it is difficult to confirm their veracity. Depending on who you choose to believe, Lee died either in Milwaukee in 1945, or drifted into obscurity and died in poverty in his home country.

Yet one question remains unanswered. If John Henry Lee was innocent of the murder of Emma Keyse, then who killed her? As it turns out there is no shortage of suspects. Chief among these is Reginald Gwynne Templer, a young lawyer who regularly visited Miss Keyse at her home. Templer's motives for these visits were less than altruistic. He was, in fact, involved in an affair with Miss Keyse's cook (and John Lee's stepsister) Elizabeth Harris. It has been suggested that, on the night of the murder, Miss Keyse came down to the servant's quarters after hearing a sound and caught Templer and Harris in the act. Templer then reacted by striking her and cutting her throat.

Backing for this theory comes from the obviously false testimony Elizabeth Harris gave at her brother's trial, evidence that contributed greatly to Lee's conviction. Was Harris protecting her lover? Or was she herself the killer? There are reports (unsubstantiated) that she confessed to the killing on her deathbed. Templer, incidentally, died of syphilis at around the time Lee was reprieved from the gallows.

Another suggestion is that Keyse was murdered by smugglers. Smuggling was rife along the South Devon coast at the time, with local fishermen reportedly involved in these clandestine activities. Emma Keyse had been engaged in a long-term dispute with locals over fishing rights. Was she killed because of it? We shall never know. Perhaps the answer is much simpler than that. Perhaps John Lee, 'The Man They Couldn't Hang,' got away with murder after all.

I Don't Like Mondays

We've all heard the song, the catchy little ditty that took Irish band, The Boomtown Rats, to the top of the charts in the summer of 1979. But behind the clever lyrics and upbeat tempo lies a far more sinister tale. The story of a disillusioned 16-year-old named Brenda Ann Spencer who decided to open fire with a .22 rifle on children playing in a San Diego schoolyard.

Brenda Ann Spencer was born on April 3, 1962, in San Diego, California. Her father, Wallace, worked as an audio-visual technician, her mother Dot was a homemaker. Her early life was by all accounts a happy one. The diminutive, freckle-faced redhead was active in sports and a good student. She was a talented photographer, winning a Humane Society award for her work. She loved animals.

But, in 1972, all of that was to change. Brenda's parents divorced, with her father gaining custody. At around the same time, she took a spill from her bicycle and hit her head, suffering a concussion.

And her personality changed. The happy, well-adjusted girl was gone. She became sullen, withdrawn and prone to violent outbursts; she began hanging with another troubled youth from the area and stories began circulating of their anti-social behavior; she became a habitual truant, a thief, a drunk and a drug user; she developed an obsession with guns and often ranted about her desire to shoot a pig (a police officer).

Brenda's home situation by this time was far from ideal. She was living with her father in virtual poverty in the San Diego suburb of San Carlos, directly across the street from Grover Cleveland Elementary School. The only furnishing in the house was a single mattress that the pair shared (Brenda would later accuse her father of sexual abuse, a charge he denied). Scattered throughout the house were empty and half-empty booze bottles.

Given these conditions, it is perhaps understandable that Brenda spent much of her time on the streets. She began racking up arrests for burglary and vandalism. In early 1978, she was arrested for shooting out the windows of the elementary school with a BB gun, a chilling foretaste of what was to come.

With a number of misdemeanors now to her name, Brenda inevitably ended up in a juvenile facility where a psychiatric evaluation determined that she was suffering from depression and potentially suicidal. Doctors recommended to Wallace Spencer that he admit his daughter to a mental hospital but he refused. Instead, he did something breathtakingly irresponsible. After discharging his daughter he took her home for the holidays. That Christmas he bought her a Ruger .22 semi-automatic rifle with a telescopic sight, throwing in 500 rounds of ammunition for good measure.

It is difficult to comprehend what Wallace Spencer was thinking when he made this gift to his daughter. It is true that both he and Brenda were firearms enthusiasts and that she was, in fact, a crack shot. Perhaps he thought that the rifle would cheer her up. Brenda would later speculate that her father had bought her the weapon in the hope that she would kill herself. Brenda Spencer chose a different path.

At around 8:30 a.m., on the morning of Monday, January 29, 1979, the school bell at Grover Cleveland Elementary sounded, summoning the children to their first class of the day. The strident tone of the bell masked the first snap of the rifle but its effects were all too evident. One of the children, standing beside a yellow bus, collapsed to the ground, bleeding. Then, as the sound of the bell faded, a clear crack was heard, echoing back off the school buildings as another child slumped to the ground. Another shot rang out, this one failing to find a target but nonetheless sparking pandemonium in the playground. Children, teachers, and parents scattered screaming in a panicked rush, the adults trying to shield their charges and guide them towards cover.

Still, the sniper continued firing, dropping one straggling child, then another. Seated in his office, school principal Burton Wragg heard the commotion and rushed immediately outside to help. He'd barely emerged from the building when a bullet struck him in the chest and he collapsed. Seeing the principal fall, school custodian Mike Suchar abandoned thoughts for his own safety and went to help, exposing himself to the sniper's bullets. He too was hit, collapsing to the tarmac beside the man he'd gone to rescue. He bled out within minutes.

Most of the students and teachers had by now made it inside the school building. Four children had been hit and the school nurse attended to their wounds as best she could. Four more injured children still lay outside and without help were likely to die of shock and blood loss unless they got help soon. Those inside the building, however, could not risk going outside. That would put them directly within the sniper's arc of fire. The sound of approaching police sirens, when it came moments later, must have sounded like blessed relief.

Crouching in the shadows of her living room across the street, Brenda Spencer watched as the first police cruiser screeched to a halt. She parted the drapes slightly with the rifle barrel, tilted her head and peered through the telescopic sight. Officer Robert Robb had just emerged from the vehicle when Spencer drew a bead on him and squeezed the trigger. She saw Robb throw up his hands to his neck and blood seep between his fingers. Then she dropped from sight, scooted down into a sitting position, her back to the wall, the rifle held upright between her knees, its barrel warm to the touch. Her breaths came in quick intakes; her mind was racing. She'd done it! She'd killed a pig!

Outside, more police cars and an ambulance had now arrived. Officer Robb (only superficially wounded despite Spencer's best efforts) quickly pointed out the direction the shots were coming from. Another officer commandeered a garbage truck and drew it across the road, cutting off the shooter's line of fire and allowing paramedics to get to the wounded.

The press had meanwhile heard about the school shooting and crews were rushing towards the scene. One enterprising journalist managed to obtain the phone number of the house now pinpointed as the sniper's nest. He dialed the number and got Spencer on the line. "Why are you doing this?" he asked, to which Spencer replied with the line that would be made famous by the song mentioned in the intro to this article. "I don't like Mondays," she said. "This livens up the day."

Twenty minutes had now passed since Brenda Spencer fired her first shot. In the schoolyard, principal Burton Wragg and custodian Mike Suchar lay dead on the ground, their bodies covered by white sheets. Eight children had been treated at the scene and were on their way to hospital. All would survive, as would police officer Robert Robb. Meanwhile, Brenda Spencer was still holed up in her house. It would take six hours of negotiation before the skinny, five-foot-two teenager laid down her rifle and gave herself up.

In the immediate aftermath of the shootings, San Diego County prosecutors stated their intention of trying Brenda Spencer as an adult, meaning that she could face a possible death sentence. Spencer's defense meanwhile, suggested that they might pursue a defense of diminished responsibility as their client was high on alcohol and angel dust at the time (a toxicology report contradicted this, showing no trace of drugs in her system).

In the end, it all proved academic. The case never came before a jury because Brenda Spencer pled guilty to two counts of first-degree murder and accepted a sentence of 25 years to life. Despite being a model prisoner, she was turned down for parole in 2005. She becomes eligible again in 2019.

The Grover Cleveland school shooting was a uniquely traumatic event in American history, the first of its kind. Little did the unwary public know that it was merely a harbinger of the far worse school massacres to come at Columbine and at Sandy Hook.

The Coffin Case

Wilbert Coffin

It is one of the most controversial cases in the annals of Canadian criminal history. Was Wilbert Coffin guilty of a brutal triple homicide, or was he the victim of a justice system determined to hold someone accountable for the murder of three tourists? Was his fate determined by inadequate counsel, or was the evidence so conclusive that the jury could do little more than rubber-stamp the prosecution's version of events? More than sixty years after the death of the main players, the questions remain. These are the facts. You decide.

Eugene Lindsey was a keen hunter. The railway steamfitter from Altoona, Pennsylvania was a fully paid up member of the 200,000-strong Pennsylvania Federation of Sportsmen's Clubs, an association for hunting and fishing enthusiasts. He had long heard stories from fellow members of the great bear hunting to be had in the unspoiled wilderness of Quebec's Gaspé region and had become determined to pay a visit. In June 1953, he realized that dream, traveling to the Gaspé with his son, Richard, 17, and

Richard's friend, Frederick Claar, aged 20. It was a trip that would end in tragedy.

The hunters arrived in Quebec in early July 1953. A few days later, on July 10, their Ford truck was found abandoned beside a road. An immediate search was launched but it would be weeks before their bodies were discovered, deep in the forest, some sixty miles from the nearest town.

Eugene Lindsey was found first, lying in a shallow stream, his remains partially consumed by animals. Given the poor condition of the corpse, it was not immediately possible to say how he'd died. Yet any idea that he might have fallen prey to the very animals he'd been stalking were quickly dispelled when a bullet graze was detected on the stock of his rifle. His wallet had also been emptied, the $600 he'd been carrying, gone. The other two victims were found about a week later, within 200 feet of each other. Both had been shot to death and their wallets emptied.

Homicide is a rarity in the Gaspé, and a triple murder was nothing short of sensational. But the attention given to this crime was unlike anything seen before in the region. Almost as soon as the news broke, US Secretary of State John Foster Dulles got on the phone to Quebec Premier Maurice Duplessis and demanded action. Duplessis, in response, dispatched his best investigator, Alphonse Matte, Quebec's chief of detectives. Matte's instructions were clear. This case needed to be resolved – and quickly.

Matte wasted little time in carrying out his remit. He'd barely arrived in Gaspé County when his attention honed in on one man, a 42-year-old mining prospector, lumberjack, and all round outdoorsman named Wilbert Coffin. Coffin was a well-known and well-liked denizen of the region, an amiable man who was always willing to lend a hand to anyone in need. It was this apparent propensity for good citizenship that elevated him to the head of the suspect list. Several people had seen him in the company of the dead men, shortly before their disappearance.

Hauled in for questioning, Coffin readily admitted to interacting with the Americans. He said that he'd initially met them on June 10 while heading into the bush to prospect for minerals. Their truck had broken down, and he drove Richard Lindsey into town to buy a new fuel pump. Thereafter, Coffin said, he drove Lindsey back to the camp, where he met the two younger members of the party. There were two other Americans in attendance, these two driving a yellow jeep.

The group all had dinner together before Coffin announced that he needed to be on his way. Before he left, Coffin promised to look in on the Lindsey party in a few days. Eugene Lindsey then peeled off three bills - a twenty and two tens - and handed them to Coffin in thanks for his assistance. Richard Lindsey gave Coffin a pocketknife to give to his young son.

The goodbyes having been said, Coffin headed into the bush. He returned a couple of days later, as he'd promised, but found the campsite deserted. Eugene Lindsey's truck was still there, however, leading Coffin to believe that the party would return. After waiting for hours, during which he consumed several alcoholic beverages, Coffin decided to leave. By now, he was quite drunk and he made the fateful decision to steal items from the campsite, including the fuel pump for the truck, several pieces of clothing belonging to Frederick Claar, and an expensive pair of binoculars.

That same night, Coffin visited a number of friends and paid off longstanding debts, using crisp new $20 U.S. bills. He also stopped off at a bar and downed several beers, again paying in U.S. currency. Somewhat the worse for wear, he drove into a ditch on the way home. When a passing vehicle stopped to help, he rewarded the helpers with a $20 bill, peeled – his beneficiaries noticed – from a thick wad of notes.

The implications were clear. Wilbert Coffin had killed and robbed the Lindsays and their friend, being none too subtle about it. When the binoculars and Frederick Claar's clothes were found in his possession, Coffin was placed under arrest on suspicion of murder. Under interrogation, he admitted to stealing the clothes but claimed that the binoculars had been a gift from the Americans. That particular claim did Coffin's cause no good. Why, investigators wondered, would the Lindsays have given such an expensive piece of equipment to a man they'd only just met, especially as they'd need it for their hunting trip. Still, despite hours of unrelenting interrogation, they failed to coerce Coffin into an admission of murder.

The case against Wilbert Coffin appeared as clear-cut as they come, the trial a mere formality. But was the evidence all that it appeared? Several commentators on the case believe not. That Wilbert Coffin was a thief there can be no doubt. He, in fact, admitted to pilfering items from the Lindsays campsite even if this admission was somewhat economical with the truth. It seems clear that Coffin also helped himself to Eugene Lindsay's bankroll and to the binoculars and Richard Lindsay's pocketknife.

But did that necessarily make him a murderer?

There is no evidence to suggest that Coffin was ever anywhere near the place where the bodies were found. Neither could ballistics tie the bullets that killed the victims to any weapon owned by Coffin. Neither was any mention made at the trial of the two Americans that had been at the Lindsay campsite. The police chose simply to ignore these potential suspects, and Coffin's lawyer did nothing to challenge them on the issue.

In fact, there was not much that defense counsel, Raymond Maher, did do at the trial. He was content simply to cross-examine the prosecution witnesses. When it came time to present his case he announced simply, "The defense rests," without calling a single witness, not even Wilbert Coffin himself.

Had the defense conducted even a cursory investigation they would have turned up adequate doubt over Coffin's guilt, if not conclusive proof of his innocence. For example, there was a note found by the police, which was not entered into evidence at the trial. This was written by one of the victims on May 13, by which time Coffin had already left the wilderness and was in Montreal. Around that same time, there were numerous sightings of the two Americans in the yellow jeep, still in the area and therefore viable suspects in the triple homicide. The defense explored neither of these grounds for reasonable doubt.

Given this woefully inadequate representation there can be little surprise that Coffin was found guilty, the jury taking just thirty minutes to convict. The judge then pronounced the mandatory sentence – death by hanging.

That sentence, of course, went on remand and was appealed all the way to the Supreme Court of Canada. During that appeal process, Coffin escaped from prison using a fake gun carved from soap. The experienced woodsman could have disappeared into Canada's vast wilderness and would probably never have been caught. Instead, his lawyer convinced him to give himself up and to put his faith in the appeals process.

That faith would prove misplaced. On February 8, 1956, the Supreme Court upheld the decision of the lower courts by a majority of 5 to 2. The following day, Wilbert Coffin died on the scaffold at the Prison de Quebec in Montreal. He is said to have gone to his death with his customary smile on his lips.

The Loss of Innocence

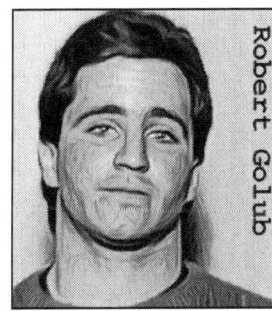

Horton Road in the village of Valley Stream, New York was a happy place to live in the 1980's, the kind of place where neighbors greeted neighbors on the streets and attended barbecues and pool parties at each other's homes; where there were communal activities and block parties; where kids played together on the streets and teenagers performed babysitting duties for each other's families. There were outsiders of course, but on Horton Road that amounted to just one family, the Golubs.

John Golub Sr. lived with his wife Elizabeth and sons Robert, 21, and John Jay, 14, in a mock Tudor house that was the most unkempt on the street. The family kept pretty much to themselves and participated in none of the community activities. Robert, unemployed and obsessed with bodybuilding, was seldom seen. John Jay was well known though, and for all the wrong reasons. He was the neighborhood bully, a habitual truant who enjoyed inflicting pain on kids half his age. For that reason alone, the local youngsters gave the house a wide berth.

One local teen who was not in the least bit afraid of John Jay Golub was 13-year-old Kelly Ann Tinyes. The Tinyes were neighbors to the Golubs and word on the street was that John Jay was sweet on Kelly. It was easy to see why. With dark blue eyes, brown hair and a smattering of freckles across her nose, Kelly was a pretty girl. She was tall for her age at five-foot-nine, and an athletically built 120 pounds.

Friday, March 3, 1989, was a frigid, blustery day on Horton Street. At the Tinyes house, Kelly, two days shy of her fourteenth birthday, was babysitting her 8-year-old brother Richard while her parents were at work at their auto body shop. Next door at the Golubs, Robert was home alone. He was sifting through the newly delivered mail, when his brother John Jay arrived, bringing with him two schoolmates. Steve Bataan and Glen McMahon had come to the Golub's home to smoke some pot.

Bataan and McMahon would have been shocked by what they saw inside the Golub house. The place was even more unkempt on the inside than it was outside. Boxes and mounds of clothing were piled everywhere; the floor was liberally scattered with trash and there were dirty dishes piled high in the kitchen sink and cluttering up the counter space. In John Jay's room, every surface was coated with dust and there were dog-eared posters hanging from the walls. Clothes spilled out from the closet and were strewn across the floor among a scattering of fast food containers, soda cans, and other trash. John Jay pointed them to a stained mattress. He lit up, took a hit and passed the joint to one of the boys. The three of them would remain where they were over the next hour, although it would later emerge that John Jay had left the room three times during that period, on each occasion for only a few minutes.

At 2:51 p.m., the phone rang at the Tinyes house. Richie, who was closest, picked it up and heard John Jay's voice on the other end. "It's John. Get Kelly," the older boy said. Richie, who like all of the other kids on the block was intimidated by John Jay, handed over the handset immediately. After that, Kelly and John Jay spoke for a short while before Kelly hung up and told her brother that she was going over to her friend Nichole's house and would be back soon. Nichole lived at number 81 Horton Road, on the other side of the Golubs.

But Kelly had told a lie to her brother. She didn't go to Nichole's but to the Golub's. Jimmy Walsh, a neighborhood boy who was six years old at the time, saw her walking up the path towards the house. Then he saw the door swing open and someone let her in, someone he later swore was John Jay.

Another neighbor, Kelly's friend Donna Callahan, also saw her enter the house, but couldn't say who had opened the door for her. Jimmy and Donna were the last people outside the Golub house to see Kelly Ann Tinyes alive.

When Richard and Victoria Tinyes arrived home later that evening, they were annoyed to find that Kelly had left her brother alone. That level of annoyance was elevated when Richie told them that Jimmy Walsh had seen her going into the Golub house. Richie and Jimmy had, in fact, gone to the house about an hour after Kelly entered. They had banged on the door but had gotten no response. Richie had also tried phoning but his call had gone unanswered. With a mixture of annoyance and apprehension, Richard and Victoria went over to their neighbor's house and knocked on the door. John Jay opened but denied that Kelly was there or had ever been there. His mother backed him up. Genuinely concerned now, the Tinyeses went back home and called the police.

At first, it was thought that Kelly might have run away from home. She had recently confided in a friend that she planned on doing just that. But with two independent witnesses having seen her enter the Golub house, that was a lead the police had to follow up. The following morning, two officers from the Nassau County PD Juvenile Aid Bureau arrived at the house and asked Elizabeth if they could carry out a search. She, in turn, phoned her husband John, who told her not to allow the officers to enter until he got there. When he arrived, he was persuaded to let the officers in. Within minutes, they'd made a horrific discovery.

Kelly Ann's body was found wrapped in a green sleeping bag and stuffed into a small, trash-filled closet in the basement. She had been hideously mutilated, her torso ripped open, her throat slashed from side to side. An autopsy would later reveal that she had been sexually assaulted and had been beaten and strangled, in addition to the knife wounds that had been inflicted upon her. The murder weapon, a 19-inch bayonet, was found inside the sleeping bag and there was another clue, a bloody handprint that would lead to the arrest of a suspect – Robert Golub.

DNA evidence would later place Golub at the crime scene and lead to his conviction for second-degree murder and a sentence of 25 years to life. Golub, however, has always maintained his innocence. But if he didn't kill Kelly Ann then who did? The only other viable suspect is his younger brother, John Jay.

It is an intriguing possibility, one that offers an undeniable thread of logic, but also creates all kinds of evidentiary problems. Evidence strongly suggests that it was John Jay who lured Kelly to the house. It was he who made the phone call (although he denies this) and it was he who was seen opening the door to Kelly (again denied). On the other hand, both Steve Bataan and Glen McMahon swear that John Jay was only out of the room for a short time, certainly not long enough to have killed and mutilated Kelly. It is also unlikely that John Jay could have subdued Kelly on his own. The muscle-bound Robert Golub however, would have had no problem doing so.

So did John Jay lure Kelly to the house for his brother to assault and kill or did he participate in the murder himself? His behavior in the immediate aftermath of the crime certainly seems suspicious. He was described as nervous and irritable and made a number of frantic calls to Bataan and McMahon in an apparent attempt to establish an alibi. He wanted his friends to tell police that they had played Nintendo until 3:45. Why was he so desperate for an alibi covering that time frame? One can only surmise.

Richard and Victoria Tinyes definitely believe that John Jay was more involved in the murder that he let on. They believe that he walked away scot-free when he should have been charged as an accessory at the very least. And they've never given up their fight for justice, launching a civil suit and recently getting the Nassau County DA to reopen the case.

Meanwhile, the Tinyes and Golub families continue to live as neighbors on Horton Street, both of them refusing to budge. It is an uncomfortable situation that has at times spilled over into open warfare, resulting in the police being called out to deal with harassment complaints on over fifty occasions in the decades since Kelly's death.

The Tinyes family still celebrates Kelly's birthday. Each year on March 5, they gather with friends and neighbors in front of their house to release pink and white balloons into the frigid winter sky. Next door, the dilapidated mock Tudor that once housed their daughter's killer clings stubbornly to its secrets.

A Blueprint For Murder

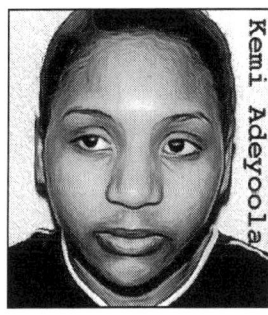

"With your butcher's knife, remove her head. Wrap it in film to contain bleeding, detach limbs one by one."

No, this is not a passage from the latest Hannibal Lecter novel. It is, in fact, an excerpt from the diary of a real psychopath, a quite horrendous treatise documenting in detail the steps required to carry out the perfect murder. Titled 'Prison and After - Making Life Count,' the document was found during a routine search at the Bullwood Hall detention center in Hockley, England in October 2004. Its author claimed that it was the first draft of a novel, although subsequent events would prove this assertion to be false. Even more shockingly, this horrific document was composed by a 17-year-old girl.

Kemi Adeyoola was born into a life of privilege. Her father is Bola Adeyoola, a former professional boxer turned millionaire property tycoon, with a reputed worth of over £10 million. The marriage between Bola and Kemi's mother Mercuria, however, was not a happy one. It ended after four years and Mercuria walked away with £4 million in compensation, as well as custody of the couple's three children.

£4 million is a considerable sum of money, certainly enough for both mother and children to have lived a comfortable lifestyle. The family, however, appeared shiftless, constantly on the move. For a time they lived in Cheltenham, then in Peterborough, and in Golders Green, London. Perhaps the reason that they moved so often was that they so frequently became involved in disputes with neighbors.

At one property in Gloucestershire, Kemi Adeyoola killed all the goldfish in a neighbor's pond. At another, she conducted a reign of terror against an Asian family, abusing their young children, attempting to poison their dog, smearing excrement on their windows, calling the mother a "Paki lover," and even attacking the father of the family, punching him in the face.

And her criminal activities were not confined to vandalism and racial slurs. By age 15, she had become a prolific shoplifter, stealing items from high street stores, later returning them with an altered receipt and demanding a refund. She boasted to her friends and siblings that shoplifting was a skill and that she was one of its foremost practitioners. But perhaps she wasn't quite as talented as she professed to be because she was eventually caught and sent to Bullwood Hall young offenders' institute for three months. It was here, with time on her hands, that Adeyoola began devising her blueprint for murder.

The document was 18 pages of neatly handwritten text. In it, Adeyoola outlined her plan to raise £3 million by finding a wealthy elderly woman, torturing her until she revealed safe combinations and bank PIN numbers, and then killing her and disposing of her body. She also compiled a list of the supplies she'd need - guns, silencers, bulletproof vests, drugs, two sharp knives, and handcuffs.

Delving deeper into the plan, Adeyoola wrote that she intended knocking on her victim's door disguised as a schoolgirl. She would claim to be a student from a nearby school doing research for a homework assignment. Having gained the victim's trust she would produce a knife and hold it to the woman's throat. Then she'd inject the victim with a tranquilizing drug and begin torturing her to extract the required information. She would then force the victim to write a letter to her husband, saying that she was leaving him. Finally, she'd kill the victim and dispose of the body. This included building a 'tent' of cling-film, in order to contain blood spatters.

The prison staff were far from convinced by Adeyoola's insistence that the document was a draft for the next crime blockbuster, but they also had no reason to believe that it was a roadmap to murder. When Adeyoola's release date rolled around she walked free. Shortly thereafter, she moved into an £800-a-month Hampstead flat with another teenager. The two of them financed this extravagance by working as escorts, reportedly earning as much as £500 a night. For Kemi Adeyoola however, that was far from enough.

In March 2005, Adeyoola's period of judicial supervision came to an end. She was now ready to put her murder scheme into action. However, she was uncertain whether she'd actually be able to go through with it. Ever the pragmatist, Adeyoola came up with a solution. She decided to carry out a trial run, targeting a 'soft' victim. That flippant decision would have horrendous consequences for one elderly London couple.

Anne and Leonard Mendel had been married for 50 years and had two children and 14 grandchildren and great grandchildren. At 84, the diminutive Anne stood just 4-foot-10 and weighed in at only 98 pounds. Yet despite her age, Anne was still active in the community and in charity work. She was devoted to her family and much loved for her willingness to always help those in need.

On the morning of March 19, Leonard Mendel left his Golders Green home to visit a nearby travel agent. He and Anne had been planning a trip to Israel to visit their daughter and were both excited about the holiday. Today was the day that he would be picking up the tickets. He arrived back at the apartment about an hour later, unaware that in the interceding 60 minutes the life he had known with his wife had been brutally ended.

Anne Mendel lay in the passageway still dressed in her pink pajamas, her body partially covered with coats from the rack. Even so, it was immediately clear that she had been badly hurt. A pool of blood had spread out around her and she did not appear to be breathing. Leonard immediately fell to his knees and started giving her CPR, breaking just long enough to call the emergency services. An ambulance was soon on the scene, but it was already too late.

The frail pensioner had suffered fourteen savage wounds from a blade five inches long and an inch wide.

The question was why? Anne Mendel had no enemies, nothing had been taken from the house, and there was no sign of sexual assault. Who would want to commit such a senseless act of violence against a defenseless woman?

The answer to that question was not long in coming. The police were able to lift DNA from under the victim's fingernails and soon had a match – to Kemi Adeyoola. Taken into custody, the teenager denied having anything to do with the murder. She explained away the DNA evidence by insisting that she had helped Mrs. Mendel cross the street the previous day and had been accidentally scratched in the process. She knew Mrs. Mendel, she said, because her family had once lived next door.

Despite her protestations of innocence, Adeyoola was charged with murder. At her trial, she appeared dressed in an expensive pinstriped suit and pink trainers. She seemed unconcerned by the gravity of her crime and spent much of the proceedings smiling and joking. She was also sticking to her story, that she hadn't murdered Anne Mendel and that her blueprint for murder was the first draft of a crime novel.

It was a story that the jury was unprepared to accept. Found guilty of murder, Kemi Adeyoola was sentenced to life in prison, with at least 20 years to be served before she becomes eligible for parole.

Fit As A Fiddle And Ready To Die

In his own mind, Kenneth Neu was a talented guy. The handsome, 25-year-old nightclub singer was determined to make it big on Broadway. The only thing was, this was the Depression and no one was hiring. Still, that didn't appear to discourage the spirited Ken. Billing himself as a "talented singer, dancer, and all-round entertainer," he spent most of his days wandering Manhattan, pestering club owners for a gig. Most often, he ended up thrown out on his butt. And on the rare occasions when his persuasive powers got him through the front door, the pay was meager, barely enough for a meal. No one ever asked him back for a repeat performance.

September 2, 1933, had been another of those dispiriting, fruitless days. As Neu emerged from the cavernous depths of a Times Square nightclub, into the drizzle of a drab fall day, he wondered if his luck was ever going to change. He began wandering aimlessly along Broadway and during that meandering struck up a conversation with a dapper stranger. The man listened sympathetically to Neu's tale of woe before formally introducing himself. His name was Lawrence Shead, and he was the owner of a string of theaters in Paterson, New Jersey. Perhaps he could be of help.

Barely able to believe his luck, Kenneth Neu gladly accepted Shead's offer of a meal. When his benefactor then suggested that they retire to his hotel suite to further discuss a "business arrangement," Neu was all too keen.

Shead however, was in no hurry to get down to formalities. He plied Neu with drink and when he thought that Neu was sufficiently relaxed, he made his move. The homosexual advance angered Neu. Not only because he disliked gays but because Shead had duped him into believing that he was interested in his career. He struck out with his fists, beating Shead to the ground and then picked up an electric iron and bludgeoned the man to death with it. He did not stop until Shead's skull was reduced to a bloody pulp.

With his victim lying dead on the carpet, Neu took a shower. Then he dressed himself in one of Shead's best suits and pocketed the dead man's well-stocked wallet. He wasn't sure if anyone had noticed him and Shead together, but decided that it was a good idea to get out of town anyway. He headed for New Orleans.

Neu quickly settled into a familiar routine in the Big Easy, pestering nightclub owners for singing gigs. But he had no better luck than he'd had in New York and with Shead's money running out, he knew he had to do something soon. He had, in the interim, met and seduced a waitress named Eunice Hotte, a married woman with a 5-year-old daughter. He'd promised to take her to

New York, telling her "We'll have a big time in the big town." Only problem was, he had not even enough money to travel to New York himself, let alone to bring his new lover along. What he did have, however, was a plan.

On the morning of Sunday, September 17, Neu told Hotte that they were leaving for New York later that day and that she should be "packed and ready to go." He then headed for a pawnshop where he hocked the watch he'd stolen from Lawrence Shead and bought a blackjack with the proceeds. His encounter with Shead had turned out fortuitously for him. Now he intended playing the ruse a second time.

Setting himself up in the lobby of the Jung Hotel, Neu began by observing the passersby. Thinning the herd like any good predator, he focused in eventually on Sheffield Clark, a 67-year-old businessman from Nashville. Sauntering over, he struck up a conversation with Clark and was unsurprised to be invited up to the man's room. Once there, he suggested a sexual liaison. When Clark agreed, Neu revealed his true intention. He threatened to report Clark to the police as a homosexual unless Clark handed over all his money.

Sheffield Clark however, was not about to be intimidated by a young punk like Kenneth Neu. He reached for the phone and asked the operator to be connected to the police. That was when Neu struck him a blow from behind. Then, with Clark lying unconscious on the floor, he wrapped the telephone cord around his neck and strangled him to death.

Neu's take from the Clark murder was $300 and, more importantly, the victim's car. Later that day, he picked up Eunice Hotte and the two set off for New York. But Neu was paranoid, fearful that once Clark's body was discovered, his car would be reported stolen. This paranoia led Neu into a fatal mistake. Somewhere along the route, he pulled over and removed the license plates. In their stead, he pasted a handwritten sign in the rear window that read: "New Car In Transit."

This, of course, was illegal, and it unsurprisingly attracted the attention of highway patrol officers. Pulled over on the Pulaski Skyway in New Jersey, Neu further aroused suspicion by giving contradictory answers to the questions he was asked. The officers then decided to take him in for further interrogation.

Despite his predicament, Neu seemed strangely upbeat as he was questioned by detectives. When one of the officers noticed brown stains on his trouser leg, Neu cheerfully admitted that it was blood. "I killed a guy in Times Square," he said. "This is his suit I'm wearing now." He then went on to admit, with a grin, that he'd committed another murder in New Orleans.

After much legal maneuvering, it was eventually decided that Neu would stand trial in Louisiana, where he was more likely to get the death penalty. Not that it seemed to bother Neu. He appeared to be lapping up all the attention he was getting. Finally, he was the star he'd always wanted to be. At the drop of a hat, he'd break into song, serenading his guards and fellow inmates, as well as members of the media. When he appeared in court for the first time, on December 12, 1933, love-struck women crammed the benches. Neu greeted them with a wink and a smile.

There were, of course, serious questions regarding Neu's sanity. His attorneys provided proof that he'd been discharged from the Army for "lunacy" and had spent time in a Georgia mental hospital. Doctors testified that he was afflicted with late stage syphilis, and was beginning to show signs of dementia.

But none of this cut any ice with the gentlemen of the jury. They deliberated for just five hours before finding Neu guilty. When the judge pronounced sentence of death, Neu thanked him by breaking into a rendition of "Sweet Rosie O'Grady."

Kenneth Neu's short time on death row was far from uneventful. He converted to Catholicism and began a fervent correspondence with a female admirer, leading him to declare, "I am passionately in love." He serenaded his fellow inmates of course and also composed some original songs, including one intended for his execution, called "Fit as a Fiddle and Ready to Hang."

He delivered a fine rendition of that tune on February 1, 1935, just before he stepped onto the gallows, wearing Lawrence Shead's suit. His last words were reportedly, "Don't muss my hair."

Missing, Presumed Dead

Lucie Blackman was fed up with life as a flight attendant. The attractive, blond, 21-year-old had been working cabin crew for British Airways for two years. The job had held for her the promise of glamor and international travel but the reality was somewhat different. Early mornings, late nights, repetitive routes and the constant jetlag had taken their toll. After two years she'd handed in her notice and quit. On March 4, 2000, she'd boarded a flight from London to Tokyo. She'd heard that there was good money to be made there, working at one of the city's many hostess clubs.

Hostess clubs are a uniquely Japanese phenomenon. Many are located in Roppongi, the neon-drenched center of Tokyo nightlife. They cater mainly to wealthy Japanese businessmen, out for a night on the town. The role of a hostess is ambivalent. They are not prostitutes (although they are free to sleep with a client if they choose). Mainly they are there to provide companionship, to make small talk, light cigarettes and pour drinks. Caucasian women are particularly popular, especially attractive blonds like Lucie

Blackman. It did not take long before she found work, at a popular Roppongi club called Casablanca.

The first few weeks were difficult for Lucie. If she'd hoped for kinder hours than she'd endured as a flight attendant she was quickly disavowed of that notion. Working hours were generally from 9 p.m. to 2 a.m., although depending on the client it might go well beyond that. The work was also boring, sitting around making conversation with strangers, many of who spoke only broken English. Lucie suffered considerably with homesickness. She told her sister via e-mail that being a hostess was like being a "flight attendant without the altitude."

The rewards, though, were considerable, up to $400 a night in salary, plus whatever gifts (financial and otherwise) the grateful client chose to add. Lucie's annual earnings at BA had been $18,700. Now she could make that in a couple of months. She decided to stick it out. It helped that she was sharing a house with a friend from England, Louise Phillips. It helped too that she had begun dating a young American Marine, Scott Fraser, currently stationed on the aircraft carrier U.S.S. Kittyhawk.

On July 1, Lucie told Louise that she was going on a dohan (a paid date) with a customer from the Casablanca. Lucie did not share the man's name, but she told Louise that he'd offered her a prepaid mobile phone if she would accompany him to a restaurant near the beach. It was a lunch date, and Lucie fully expected it to be over by early evening. She, Louise and Scott had plans to go out later that night.

At around 1:30 p.m., Lucie called Louise to let her know that she'd hooked up with her date. At around 5:00, she called again saying, "I'm being taken to the sea." Finally at 7 o'clock, she told Louise, "I'll be back in half an hour." She called Scott a few minutes later with the same message. It was the last time anyone ever heard from her.

After Lucie failed to show, Louise and Scott spent a frantic evening trying to contact her. They had still not heard from her by the following day, when Louise got a strange phone call. The man on the other end of the line spoke in a thick accent and identified himself as Akira Takagi. "Lucie has joined a newly risen cult," he said. "She is safe and training in a hut in Chiba."

Lucie's parents, Tim and Jane, first received word of their daughter's disappearance on July 3. On hearing the news, Tim immediately made plans to travel to Tokyo. So too did Lucie's younger sister, Sophie. She arrived in the Japanese capital on July 5. Tim Blackman came a few days later, after putting in place contingency plans for his construction business. Father and daughter immediately got to work, printing and distributing 30,000 Missing Person posters. They talked to Lucie's friends and acquaintances. They called a press conference. They met with police.

But if the Blackmans had hoped for an urgent response from the authorities, they were disappointed. The police seemed almost disinterested in pursuing the case. When Tim suggested that they trace the three cell phone calls Lucie had made on the day she disappeared, they demurred, citing privacy laws and technical limitations. Tim also asked why the police had not questioned the owner of the Casablanca club, to find out the name of Lucie's final date. He got no answer to his question.

It is a testimony to Tim and Sophie's determination that despite these considerable roadblocks they never gave up. Indeed, they were about to receive help from a very high profile source. Sir Richard Branson, founder and CEO of Virgin Enterprises, got to hear of Lucie's disappearance via a friend of Tim's, a limo driver who had often driven Branson. He immediately offered to help, setting up an office in Tokyo, with an information hotline staffed by British ex-pats. Yet despite a reward of £100,000, offered by an unnamed British businessman, the clues regarding Lucie's disappearance arrived in a trickle, rather than the deluge Tim and Sophie hoped for.

Back in Britain, Jane Blackman had not been idle in the hunt for her daughter. A barrage of phone calls and e-mails were directed to the British foreign office, eventually working their way up to Prime Minister Tony Blair. As it turned out, Blair was due in Japan on July 21 to attend the G-8 summit in Okinawa. There, he raised the issue of Lucie's disappearance with his Japanese counterpart, Yoshiro Mori. The result was immediate. As if by magic, the privacy and technical issues that the police had cited disappeared and the investigation stepped up several gears. The Tokyo Police would eventually assign more officers to the Blackman case than it had to the 1995 sarin gas attack on the city subway system.

And there was momentum too from the information hotline. Three foreign women came forward to relate remarkably similar stories. Each of them had been working at hostess clubs and had gone on a dohan with a wealthy, well-dressed Japanese businessman. Each had been taken to a seaside restaurant and had woken later at their host's apartment with no recollection of how they'd got there or what had happened to them. Had something similar happened to Lucie? And if so, where was she?

The answer to that question moved a step closer on October 12 when the police arrested a 48-year-old Japanese businessman named Joji Obara. Of Korean descent, Obara had been born in Osaka, Japan in 1952. His family was dirt poor but through determination and hard work his father had worked himself up from being a scrap metal collector to owning a string of amusement arcades. This had allowed Obara to attend some of Japan's most prestigious schools and also to inherit a fortune when his father died in 1969. Obara later attended Keio University, graduating with degrees in law and politics. After graduation, he became a naturalized Japanese citizen and legally changed his name from the native Korean, Kim Sung Jong, to Joji Obara. Then he set about expanding on his already substantial fortune.

It was the early 80's and Japan was thriving. Seeking to cash in, Obara set up an investment company and began speculating in real estate. At first, he did well. But he'd got in relatively late in the game and when the market crashed it took down Obara's fortune with it. Had it not been for Obara's mother, he would likely have ended up destitute. She reportedly paid over $30 million to his various creditors.

Yet despite these catastrophic losses, Obara's extravagant lifestyle appeared unaffected. He held onto his seaside condo, was still chauffeured around in his beloved red Rolls Royce, still maintained his collection of Ferraris, Maseratis and Aston Martins.

Rumor had it that Obara's company was being used as a front for the Sumiyoshi organized crime syndicate.

If Obara had one other passion it was the hostess clubs. He appeared obsessed with Western women and with blondes in particular. It was he who was the wealthy businessman identified by the three callers to the hotline. As the world was about to discover, that was just the tip of the iceberg.

At first, Obara denied any involvement in Lucie Blackman's disappearance, denied even knowing her. But the evidence found at his house told a very different story. There were journals and audio diaries containing entries that implicated him in myriad sexual assaults on women; there were more than a dozen different varieties of drugs including sleeping pills and chloroform; there were blond hairs that would later be matched to Lucie Blackman; there was a roll of film containing pictures of Lucie; and there was a collection of videotapes, all of them showing Obara having sex with women who appeared unconscious or semi-conscious.

And then there was the testimony of the women who had survived being date raped by Obara. All of them told a similar story. How he'd met them at hostess clubs, invited them on dohans, drove them to the sea and lured them to his home.

Once there he would invariably invite them to taste a rare wine that he'd just acquired. When some of the women complained about the bitter taste, he said that it was because the wine was infused with special herbs.

The victim would have no recall of what happened next, but Obara's video collection filled in the sickening detail. They showed Obara having sex with his victims, sodomizing them, and penetrating them with various objects. He is shown on a number of the tapes applying a chloroform soaked cloth to the victim's mouth and nose. The woman would wake 24 to 48 hours later, feeling sick and disorientated. Obara would tell her that she had consumed an entire bottle of vodka and passed out.

Little did these women know that they were the lucky ones. At least one young hostess, 21-year-old Australian model Carita Ridgeway, did not survive Obara's deadly attentions. In 1992, Obara had staggered into Hideshima Hospital dragging a gravely ill Carita with him. He told hospital staff that she'd had a bad reaction to shellfish. When Carita died a few days later, her death was erroneously attributed to liver failure as a result of eating tainted seafood. Now, eight years after her death, it seemed impossible to prove otherwise.

But investigators were about to receive a much-needed break. Carita's liver had, in fact, been preserved after the initial autopsy. Now retested, it revealed the awful truth. Carita Ridgeway had died due to toxic levels of chloroform in her liver. Obara, still protesting his innocence over Lucie Blackman, was charged with causing her death.

For the Blackmans, Obara's arrest was a bittersweet victory. They now firmly believed that the man behind their daughter's disappearance was in custody. However, they still had no idea where Lucie was, or what had happened to her.

The signs did not look good. It emerged that, late on the night of July 2, Obara had called several hospitals in the area, asking for advice on how to treat a victim of a drug overdose. On July 3, he'd purchased a chainsaw, a bag of cement and a shovel from a hardware store near his condo. That same afternoon, the manager of the condominium complex reported to police that one of his tenants was behaving suspiciously. Officers were dispatched to Obara's apartment and found him with his hands coated in wet cement. He agreed to let them have a look around but promptly changed his mind when they tried to enter the bathroom. The officers then departed. They later filed a report and left it at that.

It would be January 2001 before the Tokyo police finally decided to search the area around Obara's condo. It produced almost immediate results.

Lucie Blackman's badly decomposed corpse was found buried in a seaside cave just a few hundred yards from where Jogi Obara lived. The body had been cut into eight pieces, the head shaved and encased in a block of concrete. Because of the advanced state of decomposition, it was impossible to determine cause of death and Obara (who claimed she'd died of a drug overdose) was therefore never convicted of her murder.

He was, however, found guilty of the manslaughter of Carita Ridgeway, as well as multiple rapes. On April 24, 2007, Obara was sentenced to life in prison. He continues to deny any involvement in the death of Lucie Blackman.

In League With Satan

Everyone knew that Ricky Kasso was crazy. The teenaged 'Acid King' had done so much LSD, smoked so much Angel Dust, that it had turned his brain to jelly. When he was high, he'd walk deep into the Aztakea Woods, outside of Northport, Long Island, to converse with Satan. He said that the Devil appeared to him as a glowing tree. On other occasions, he went to the local cemetery to smoke up. He'd recently been arrested for digging up a corpse. No, you didn't want to mess with crazy Ricky. Gary Lauwers found that out the hard way.

Gary and Ricky had been friends, fellow dustheads who enjoyed getting stoned together. That was until Rick passed out at a party and Gary rifled through his pockets and stole ten bags of Angel Dust. Problem was that he'd done so in front of witnesses. When Ricky later confronted him, he returned five of the little yellow envelopes that contained the drugs. He promised to pay for the other, the five he'd used, but he was slow in doing so. Bad mistake. Bad, bad, bad mistake.

At first, Ricky resorted to standard intimidation methods. He tracked Gary down and along with his friends, Jimmy Toriano and Albert Quinones, beat him senseless. When that didn't work, he repeated the remedy – three more times. Eventually, he threatened to kill Gary if he did not come up with the money. It was a threat that Gary took seriously. Soon after, he began telling friends that Ricky was going to murder him. He started carrying a hunting knife for protection. He also began making a concerted effort to scrape together the fifty bucks that he owed. Eventually, he handed it over, leading to Ricky calling a truce. "What's a few bags of dust compared to a good friend?" he told Gary.

June 16, 1984, was a warm evening in Northport. Ricky Kasso, dressed in an AC/DC t-shirt, was trawling the streets with Jimmy Toriano and Albert Quinones, pushing drugs to his teenaged clientele. And there were plenty of those around, school had only recently let out and the Northport teens were in the mood to party.

One of those out on the town that night was Gary Lauwers. Earlier in the evening he'd visited a female friend and told her of his plans to quit the drugs, finish school and eventually go to college. By the time he encountered Kasso, Toriano, and Quinones, however, Lauwers was high as a kite. When Kasso suggested they go into the Aztakea woods to smoke some dust, he readily agreed.

We know what happened in the woods that night only because of the testimony of Albert Quinones, who agreed to turn State's evidence in exchange for immunity from prosecution. According to Quinones' version of events, the foursome walked deep into the woods to find a spot to get high. Once they located a suitable place, they took a few hits of the mescaline that Kasso had brought along, then decided to build a fire. At this stage, Ricky and Gary were talking and laughing together, just like the friends they'd always been.

With a pile of logs and kindling gathered for the fire, Ricky tried to get a blaze going. But the wood was damp due to recent rains and wouldn't ignite. Gary then took off his socks and set them alight, succeeding briefly in getting a small fire started.

This, however, did not last long. As the flame died, Ricky, in a more menacing tone, suggested that Gary burn the denim jacket he was wearing. "How about I just use the sleeves?" Gary said, removing the jacket. He then produced his hunting knife and hacked the sleeves from the jacket, set them alight and got a small fire blazing. But this too, was soon reduced to embers and Ricky then suggested that Gary cut off some of his hair and throw it on the fire.

The tension now, despite the drugs they'd taken, was obvious. Gary got slowly to his feet, seemingly ready to flee at any moment. "I have funny vibes that you're going to kill me," he said.

"What?" Ricky responded. "Are you crazy? I'm not going to kill you."

And perhaps, up until that moment, he hadn't really considered killing Gary. Perhaps Gary's premonition was what actually triggered the attack. Whatever the case, Ricky suddenly launched himself at Gary. He was bigger and stronger, given additional strength by the mescaline he'd taken. Still, Gary put up a valiant fight. As they rolled on the ground, he broke free and made a run for it, gaining a few yards before Jimmy Toriano tackled him to the ground. Then Kasso was on top of him, using his teeth to tear at his victim, ripping a chunk of flesh from his throat, severing an earlobe. Meanwhile, Toriano joined the attack, using his boots on Gary's ribs.

Still, Kasso wasn't done. Retrieving Gary's hunting knife from the ground, he began stabbing him, inflicting several deep wounds. Then he pulled his helpless victim to his feet. "Say you love Satan," Kasso demanded, speaking directly into Gary's bloodied face.

"I love my mother," Gary rasped, something that appeared to infuriate Kasso. He launched another attack with the knife, stabbing Gary again and again, inflicting a total of 32 wounds to his chest, neck and face. Eventually, he allowed his victim to slump to the forest floor.

But Lauwers was not yet dead, and neither was his suffering over. Before he eventually expired from his horrendous injuries, Kasso inflicted some more. Gary was burned, slashed across the face and had his eyes gouged. Death, when it came, must have seemed like a mercy. Kasso and Toriano then dragged the body deeper into the woods, covered it with leaves and walked away.

In the aftermath of the murder, Kasso and Toriano fled to Saratoga Springs, fearing arrest. They needn't have worried. Gary Lauwers was a habitual runaway and his friends and family assumed that he'd hit the road again. No one reported him missing. The only other person who knew about the murder was Albert Quinones, and he was hardly about to rat out his buddies. In fact, when Kasso phoned him a couple of days later, Quinones told him that there was no heat at all over Gary's disappearance and that it was safe to return to Northport.

Had Rick Kasso been able to keep his mouth shut, he might well have gotten away with murder. But the Acid King was never likely to do that. Keen to impress his teenaged hangers-on, he began boasting about the murder he'd committed, "in the name of Satan." He even added some embellishments, insisting that he'd heard a crow caw in the moment that Gary Lauwers died. This he took to be a sign from Satan, giving his approval for the murder.

It was a tale that Kasso told several times over the weeks that followed. If anyone expressed doubts about his story, he'd invite them into the woods to view Gary's decomposing remains. A number of Northport teenagers took him up on that offer, tramping deep into the Aztakea to satisfy their morbid interest. And yet, remarkably, not one of them went to the authorities. It was only when a friend of Gary's heard the stories via the grapevine that the truth came out.

After receiving an anonymous tip-off the police sent canine units into the Aztakea woods on July 4, 1984. It wasn't long before the dogs picked up a scent and led their handlers to the badly decomposed corpse. The notches clearly visible on the exposed ribcage left no doubt as to how he'd died.

Ricky Kasso, Jimmy Toriano and Albert Quinones were taken into custody on July 5. Under questioning, Kasso had no problem admitting to the murder. In fact, he did so in such an upbeat tone that investigators should perhaps have been concerned about his state of mind. He should probably have been placed on suicide watch. Instead, he was returned to his cell where, on July 7, 2004, he hung himself. His co-accused, Jimmy Toriano, was later acquitted of second-degree murder.

The aftermath of Gary Lauwers' murder brought forth wild speculation about its occult connections. This was after all the eighties and "Satanic panic" was at its height in America. Was Ricky Kasso really inspired to kill by his satanic beliefs? It's doubtful. The only connection that could be found to any devil-worshipping activities was a loose affiliation with the so-called 'Knights of the Black Circle,' a bunch of high school kids involved in séances and animal sacrifice. There was also speculation that Kasso was influenced by his love of Heavy Metal music, especially the 'satanic' lyrics of his favorite band AC/DC. This is a quite ludicrous suggestion. The only song in the band's repertoire that appears to hint at 'Satanism' is Hell's Bells, a tongue-in-cheek swipe at those accusing them of writing satanically influenced material.

The truth is that Ricky Kasso was the classic case of a young life lost to addiction. He'd once been a bright student and a talented athlete, but his involvement with drugs had put an end to that. It had also led him down the path to murder.

Bonfire Night

November 5th is Bonfire Night in Britain, an occasion on which Brits commemorate the failed 1605 plot by Guy Fawkes to assassinate King James I by blowing up the Houses of Parliament. Traditionally, these celebrations are characterized by bonfires and fireworks, and so it was that on the evening of November 5, 1930, cousins William Bailey and Alfred Brown attended a party where the amusements included various pyrotechnic displays.

In the early hours of the following morning, the cousins were walking home along a darkened path when they spotted a fierce blaze in the distance. They'd barely had time to take in the scene when a man came hustling along the path towards them. "What's going on?" one of the cousins asked.

"Looks like someone's had a bonfire," the man replied as he hurried past and disappeared into the darkness.

That assessment, as it turned out, was incorrect. As the cousins approached, they could clearly see that the source of the blaze was a burning automobile. Fortunately, no one appeared to be at the wheel, but the fire was so fierce that they could not get close enough to verify if anyone else was inside. Instead, they ran to the nearby village of Hardingstone and raised the alarm.

By the time the village constable arrived at the scene, the flames had subsided somewhat, allowing him to get a closer look at the wreck. To his horror, he saw a severely burned body slumped across the front seat. And now that he'd spotted the corpse, he registered the smell of it, the stench of broiling flesh overlaid with the acrid tang of rubber from the vehicle's tires. Then came the clanking bell of an approaching fire truck and moments later, the crew got to work dousing the flames. It would be nearly 4 a.m. before the body could be retrieved from the wreckage and removed to Northampton General Hospital for autopsy. Such was the ferocity of the fire that a leg and an arm had been entirely burned away from the corpse.

Initially, it was assumed that the fire had been a tragic accident. But as the police began sifting through the cooling remains of the vehicle, they discovered something that roused their suspicions. It was a metal jerry can, burned almost beyond recognition. Combined with the report of the man seen rushing away from the scene, it perhaps suggested that this was not an accident after all. Perhaps something more sinister was at play. The only way to find out was to track down the mysterious stranger.

But that was easier said than done. The witnesses, Bailey and Brown, had caught only a fleeting glance of the man, and in poor light at that. They described him as about five-foot-ten, with a roundish face, a small mustache and black curly hair. He was well dressed and carrying a briefcase. Officers were dispatched to every hotel and boarding house in the area but found no one who'd seen a man answering to that description.

The police had better luck identifying the victim of the fire. The vehicle had been registered to a man named Alfred Arthur Rouse, a traveling salesman from Finchley, London. When officers called at his home, his wife Lily tearfully identified a belt buckle and a swatch of charred cloth from his jacket. Yes, those look like Alfred's, she sobbed, and no, she didn't know of anyone who might have wanted to cause him harm. He was a good man and a wonderful husband.

The police were now faced with a problem. They had a victim of an apparent homicide and not even the smidgen of a lead on the perpetrator. It appeared, even at this early stage, that the case would go unsolved. Then, entirely out of the blue, came a phone call that would turn the investigation on its head.

The call was from the police in Cardiff to lead investigator Detective Sergeant Skelly of Scotland Yard. According to the Cardiff Police, a Miss Phyllis Jenkins had seen the story in the newspaper and reported that Alfred Rouse was the boyfriend of her sister, Ivy. Rouse, she said, had been visiting Ivy in Wales over the last few days and had only just boarded a bus for London.

The lead seemed far from promising, especially as the police believed Rouse to be dead. Nonetheless, DS Skelly was there to meet the bus when it pulled into Victoria Bus Station on November 7. To his surprise, he spotted a man matching the exact description of his suspect, alighting from the bus. Confronted by Skelly and another plainclothes officer, the man identified himself as Alfred Rouse, owner of the burned out vehicle. "I'm glad it's over," he said. "I haven't been able to sleep."

But if Skelly took those words as a confession to murder, he was soon to be disappointed. Taken to Hammersmith Police Station, Rouse issued a statement in which he insisted that the blaze had been an accident. According to him, he'd picked up a man hitchhiking on the Great North Road. They had traveled together for a while, but as they approached Hardingstone the vehicle had started to "misfire." Rouse had assumed that they were running low on gas and as he needed to relieve himself anyway, he pulled over. Before heading into the bushes, he'd asked the man to fill the tank from the fuel canister he was carrying. Moments later, while standing in the bushes several yards away, he'd heard an explosion.

Rouse had run back to the car and seen that it was on fire, with the man trapped inside. He'd tried to open the door but had been driven back by the flames. Panicked and believing that he would be held responsible for the man's death, he had fled the scene, encountering William Bailey and Alfred Brown as he did so. Asked how he thought the fire might have started, Rouse speculated that his passenger must have been smoking a cigarette while filling the gas tank. There was only one problem with that theory. Why then had the man been found inside the vehicle? Alfred Rouse could offer no answer.

The interrogation had gone on for over four hours and it did not take a genius to conclude that Alfred Rouse was not telling the truth. What the police couldn't figure out was motive. Why had Rouse chosen to murder a man that he had only just met? Had there been some sort of homosexual encounter between them? Had Rouse rejected the man's overtures, or had his own advances been turned down? Had that led to an altercation? Rouse seemed affronted by the idea. He was most certainly not queer, he said, quite the opposite. In fact, he had several mistresses. "But it's an expensive game," he sighed. "My harem takes me all over the country."

As the police would later find out, Rouse's claims were not an exaggeration. The foppish, conceited commercial traveler appeared to be irresistible to certain women. During his years on the road he'd racked up over eighty affairs, had been married bigamously several times and had fathered a number of children. But his dalliances came at a cost, placing an enormous financial strain on his meager resources. Eventually, Rouse had decided to clean the slate and start over. He'd hatched a plan whereby he could stage his own death and disappear. In order to do so, he needed a corpse to substitute for his own.

But whatever his other faults, Rouse was not a violent man. The thought of actually killing someone horrified him and he pushed it to the back of his mind, an intriguing thought, but one that he was never going to take action on. That is until November 5, when an opportunity suddenly presented itself.

Rouse had been en route to Leicester and had stopped off at the Swan and Pyramid pub in Whetstone. There, he encountered a man and struck up a conversation with him. The man said that he was unemployed and had been hitchhiking from town to town looking for work. A few drinks later and the man revealed a crucial piece of information. He was alone in the world, he said, unmarried and with no living relatives.

The plot that had been festering for so long in Albert Rouse's brain percolated now to the surface. Here, sitting right in front of him, was the answer to all his problems. There and then he decided that this was it, another opportunity might never present itself. Before he left to visit one of his many lovers, he told the man that he was driving on to Leicester later that evening and asked if he could offer him a lift. The stranger (whose name Rouse never learned) gratefully accepted.

At around 8 a.m., Rouse returned to the Swan to pick up his passenger. He was carrying with him a gift for his new friend, a bottle of whiskey. The man immediately broke the seal and started chugging the liquor straight from the bottle. By the time they reached Hardingstone, at around two in the morning, he was snoring away in the passenger seat.

Rouse pulled the car to the side of a quiet road then shook his passenger awake and asked if he needed to relieve himself. The man muttered that he did and staggered from the vehicle, making for the bushes. He hadn't yet reached them when Rouse walked up behind him and struck him on the head with a wooden mallet.

The man collapsed without a sound. Rouse then dragged him back to the vehicle and propped him up in the driver's seat. He immediately slid sideways but Rouse didn't bother righting him again. Instead, he hauled the jerry can from the back of the vehicle, opened it and started pouring gasoline over the unconscious man and over the vehicle itself. Then he struck a match and watched as fire took hold. He walked away as his recent acquaintance was being burned alive.

Alfred Rouse might well have gotten away with murder had he not encountered William Bailey and Alfred Brown almost immediately after setting the fire. As it was, he found himself on trial for his life at Northampton Assizes in January 1931. The case against him was substantive, with expert prosecution witnesses proving forensically that the fire had been deliberately set. Against that testimony, Rouse's assertion that the victim must have opened the jerry can inside the car and then struck a match, was easily exposed as a lie. In the end, it took the jury just 15 minutes to find Rouse guilty of murder. The judge took even less than that the sentence him to death.

Alfred Arthur Rouse died on the gallows at Bedford Jail on March 10, 1931. His staunchest supporter to the end was his much-wronged wife, Lily.

Dancing With The Reaper

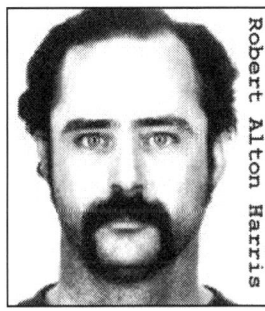

The State of California had not carried out an execution in 25 years, not since the U.S. Supreme Court had ruled the death penalty unconstitutional in 1972. The ruling had, of course, been reversed in 1976, and many states had soon thereafter begun putting condemned inmates to death. Not California though. Although the state's judges continued to hand down death sentences, swelling inmate numbers at San Quentin, it had been over two decades since any of those sentences had been carried out. Today, Tuesday, April 21, 1992, that was to change.

The condemned man was Robert Alton Harris, convicted of the 1978 murder of two teenagers. Arrested along with his younger brother within hours of the double homicide, Harris was subsequently sentenced to death. He would spend the next 14 years appealing his conviction but all of those options had been exhausted now. The governor had turned down an appeal for clemency. The execution was going ahead.

At precisely 4 a.m., Harris was removed from the death cell and marched the fifteen paces from there to the gas chamber. He was dressed in jeans and a blue prison shirt, his demeanor neutral, his posture slightly bowed. Two prison guards got to work strapping him into one of the two wooden chairs that stood in the center of the chamber. They'd just finished their work when word came that an appellate judge had granted a further stay. Harris was then unbuckled and led back to his cell by the guards.

The reprieve, though, was short-lived. Within two hours, the Supreme Court had overturned the appeal judge's order. By 6 a.m., Harris was back in the chamber. Five minutes later the door was sealed. Forty-nine witnesses stood watching the man on the other side of the glass. He was breathing heavily, almost hyperventilating, his mouth moving, forming the words "I'm sorry."

How had it come to this? How had Robert Harris ended up as the first man in California's gas chamber in nigh on a quarter century?

Robert Alton Harris was born three months prematurely on January 15, 1953, his early entry into the world facilitated by a kick from his father, directed at his heavily pregnant mother's stomach. Somehow, the frail infant managed to survive that violent introduction, but it provided just a foretaste of what was to come. Both of his parents were alcoholics. Both made a habit of taking their frustrations out on their children. At age two, Robert had his jaw shattered by his father's fists. On another occasion, his father drove a fork through his tiny hand, after he reached for something on the dinner table without asking for permission first.

Another of Harris senior's favorite pastimes was to instruct his children to hide and then hunt them down with a loaded gun. He promised to shoot anyone who he found. Given his state of perpetual inebriation, it is a wonder that he never carried through on that threat. He was eventually sent to prison for sexually molesting his daughters. By then, Robert's mother was well on her way to drinking herself to an early grave. By his teens, the boy himself was a heavy drinker and already falling foul of the law. He was sanctioned for killing neighborhood pets, then served three years in a juvenile facility for petty larceny and auto theft.

Robert Harris, it seemed, was intent on self-destruction and the destruction of anyone who crossed his path. One of the unfortunates who found himself in that position was James Wheeler. Wheeler and his wife had been sharing a home with Harris' brother Ken, when an altercation occurred between him and Harris. During the fight that followed, Harris beat Wheeler to a pulp, then sprayed him with lighter fluid and set him alight.

Arrested for murder, Harris claimed that he had acted to protect Wheeler's wife, after Wheeler threatened to stab her with a knife. At the subsequent trial, Mrs. Wheeler backed up this story, although she later admitted that she had done so only because Harris had threatened to kill her if she testified against him. Harris eventually copped a deal to involuntary manslaughter. He would serve just three years for the sadistic murder before being paroled in 1978. That same year, he would commit the crime that catapulted him to infamy, and ultimately to the gas chamber.

In June 1978, Harris approached his younger brother Daniel with a plan for a bank heist he wanted to carry out. All he needed, he said, was a couple of weapons. Keen to be in on the action, Daniel said that he knew where they could get some. His neighbor Jim Corbin had a .22 rifle and a .9-millimeter Luger pistol. That same night, while Corbin was out, the brothers broke into his house and liberated the firearms.

On the evening of June 2, Robert and Daniel drove from their home in Visalia, California to San Diego. The next morning, they bought some ammunition and then drove to a rural area outside Mira Mesa, where they practice fired the weapons and also ran through some drills for the bank robbery. The following day they purchased more ammunition and some ski masks. All they needed now was a getaway vehicle. On the morning of July 5, the day of their planned heist, they spotted one.

Michael Baker, 16, and his best friend John Mayeski, 15, had driven to the mall on Mira Mesa Boulevard to pick up some hamburgers. They were sitting in Michael's green Ford eating their food when a man approached, pulled out a gun and pointed it at them. "Play along and nobody gets hurt," he said. Then he slipped into the backseat and ordered Michael to drive. As the car pulled away the man turned and looked out of the rear window. Michael, consulting his mirror, saw another car following them. "Keep going towards Miramar Lake," the man instructed. Left no other choice, Michael obeyed.

At the lake, Michael was instructed to drive to a remote fire trail, the same spot where the Harris brothers had practiced their marksmanship the previous day. Now Daniel Harris pulled up behind them and got out of his vehicle holding a rifle. "Don't worry," he assured the frightened teens, "Everything's going to be alright."

Michael and John were asked if they had any rope in the car and said that they did not. They were then forced at gunpoint to walk up the steep fire trail. As they walked Robert Harris explained why they had been abducted. He and his brother were going to commit a bank robbery, he said, and they needed Michael's car as a getaway vehicle. The boys both said that they were willing to cooperate and would not cause any trouble. Michael suggested that Harris should take them to the top of the hill and leave them there. By the time they made their way back to town, he said, the robbery would have been carried out and the brothers would be long gone. He even promised that he and John would give the police misleading descriptions of the abductors.

Robert Harris agreed that this would be a good idea. The group started climbing the hill, Daniel Harris in front, the boys in the middle, Robert Harris bringing up the rear. They'd traveled only a short distance when Daniel heard a shot.

Daniel swung around just in time to see John Mayeski collapse to the ground. Then, as the other captive fled into the brush, Robert Harris stood over the fallen boy and cold-bloodedly shot him in the head. Robert then set off after Michael Baker. Finding the boy crouched behind a tree, he raised his pistol. "Quit crying and die like a man," he told Michael. Then, when the boy started to pray, "God can't help you now, boy. You're going to die." Harris then fired four times, aiming for the head. Finally, he walked over and pumped another bullet into John Mayeski's prone form before heading casually back down the hill. "You coming or what?" he called over his shoulder to his stunned brother.

Back at the vehicles, Robert slid into the passenger seat and instructed his brother to get behind the wheel. The burgers that the boys had been eating lay discarded in the foot well and Harris picked them up and started chomping on them. He offered one to Daniel but Daniel refused, something that Robert found highly amusing. "No point letting good food go to waste," he chuckled.

During the rest of the short journey into Mira Mesa Robert giggled constantly while relating how he'd shot the boys and imagining the reactions of their families once they heard the news of their sons' deaths. Daniel could see flecks of blood and flesh on his brother's face, blowback from the point-blank shots he had fired at his young victims.

Finally, they reached Mira Mesa and Robert directed Daniel to the bank he intended holding up, just across the street from where they had encountered Michael Baker and John Mayeski. The robbery went exactly as planned, but unfortunately for Robert Harris, one of the bank customers recognized him and later passed on his name to the police. At 1 p.m. that same day, the brothers were arrested at their home. One of the arresting officers, ironically, was Michael Baker's father, who at that point was still unaware of his son's murder.

But that would soon change. Within hours of the arrest, Daniel Harris broke down and confessed to the double homicide, pointing his brother out as the shooter. After being confronted with

Daniel's tape-recorded admission, Robert Harris admitted to the murders. "Yeah, I shot them," he sneered. "So what?"

Later, Harris would offer conflicting reasons for shooting the boys. To his sister he claimed that he had shot them because he wanted to die and knew that he would get the death penalty for the crimes. To a fellow con, he provided a more plausible explanation. "I couldn't have no punks running around that could identify me," he said, "So I wasted them."

By the time the matter came to trial, however, Harris was singing a different tune altogether. He now claimed that he had not committed the murders at all and had only confessed to protect the real shooter, his brother Daniel. The jury did not believe him, finding him guilty of first-degree murder and recommending the death penalty. That penalty was now about to be carried out.

By order of a federal judge, a camera had been mounted on a tripod and stood outside the execution chamber, facing in on Robert Alton Harris, the purpose being to establish whether Harris had suffered unnecessarily during his execution.

At 6:05 a.m., the order was given. A prison official depressed the lever that slowly lowered the sodium cyanide pellets into the small vat of sulfuric acid that sat beneath the chair. A lethal fog of hydrocyanic gas immediately began rising from the vat. Harris took in a number of deep breaths. Within seconds he began to gasp and twitch convulsively. His head snapped back and he strained against the straps. Then his body relaxed and his slumped forward, his mouth lax and open, his face turning an unearthly shade of blue. There was a final cough and a spasmodic convulsion and then Robert Harris moved no more. Eleven minutes after the start of the procedure he was pronounced dead by Warden Daniel Vasquez.

Vasquez later shared Harris' final words with the media, taken from a line spoken by actor Keanu Reeves in the movie, Bill and Ted's Excellent Adventure: "You can be a king or a street sweeper, but everyone dances with the grim reaper."

The Devil In Petticoats

As insurance frauds go, this one was pretty audacious. Emil Marek had decided to chop off his leg in order to claim against an accident policy. The plan was to make it look like the axe had slipped while he was cutting wood, but after striking the initial blow, Marek collapsed in agony. The cut had inflicted a deep gash on his shin, but it was not enough for his purposes. He, therefore, through gritted teeth, instructed his young wife Martha to finish the job. She delivered two more strikes on the damaged appendage, then rushed to call the doctor.

Emil Marek was transported to the hospital at Moedling, where it was determined that the leg hung on by no more than a sinew. It would have to be amputated. The following day, June 13, 1925, Mrs. Marek contacted the Anglo-Danubian Lloyd Company in Vienna and lodged a claim against the $400,000, policy. The insurers were not pleased. Marek had only bought the policy a week earlier and had paid only one premium. They launched an inquiry and soon learned from the surgeon who had performed Emil's amputation that the injury could not have occurred the way the Mareks described it. There were, in fact, three distinct cuts to the shin. What man would have the fortitude to hack three times into his own shin with an axe?

The insurance claim was thus rejected. Not only that, but the Mareks found themselves charged with fraud.

The trial was set for December 1926. But the Mareks were not about to give up their windfall without a fight. Roping in the help of a hospital orderly, Karl Mraz, they concocted a new plan. Mraz was bribed to testify that he'd seen a doctor at the hospital inflict two additional wounds on the severed shinbone, the implication being that the doctor was on the payroll of the insurance company.

The deception might well have worked, but then Mraz got greedy and demanded more money. When the Mareks refused, he went to the police and reported their attempt to bribe him. The Mareks now found themselves arrested for the additional charge of bribery.

After several delays, the trial eventually got underway on March 28, 1927. Public opinion was staunchly behind the Mareks, who were deemed to be the victims of a big corporation's strong-arm tactics. Perhaps mindful of this, the insurance company agreed to an out-of-court settlement of $50,000. But most of that was gobbled up by the Marek's legal fees, and they still had a bribery charge to face. Found guilty on that charge, they were each sentenced to four months in prison, although given the amount of time they'd already spent in custody, they were released immediately.

It was a victory of sorts, but the harsh reality was that the Mareks had gained just $6,000 from a scheme that had left Emil an invalid. And that windfall was quickly whittled away on a series of hair-brained business schemes. By 1930, the couple was destitute again, and they now had the additional burden of a child to feed.

In 1932, Martha gave birth to a second child and the family was forced to move from their Moedling villa to a far less salubrious neighborhood. Adding to their woes, Emil became ill in early July and was dead by the end of the month, apparently of tuberculosis. Martha Marek cashed in an insurance policy on his life, and another when her baby daughter, Ingeborg, died on September 2. Her son, Alfons, also became ill but recovered, probably because Martha had identified a more lucrative target.

Suzanne Lowenstein was Martha Marek's great-aunt, the 67-year-old widow of an army officer. In the spring of 1934, Martha reached out to Mrs. Lowenstein, offering to care for her in her old age. The old lady was flattered by the interest, and so impressed by Martha's devoted care, that she quickly made her the sole beneficiary of her estate. Within a month she was dead and Martha became the proud own of a well-appointed home on the Kuppelwiesergasse.

Martha Marek however, had never had a head for money and it wasn't long before this latest windfall had been sufficiently eroded, so that she had to take in boarders. One of those was an insurance agent named Jens Neumann, who became her lover; another was a 53-year-old seamstress named Felicitas Kittenberger.

In short order, Martha had prevailed upon Neumann to write a life insurance policy on Mrs. Kittenberger, with Martha as the sole beneficiary. Then a familiar pattern of events unfolded. Mrs. Kittenberger became ill, her eyesight failed, she lost the use of her limbs, her hair began falling out. By June 2 she was dead. Four days later Marek collected a cash payment of $785.

Kittenberger's relatives, however, were not about to let the matter lie. Her son Herbert, in fact, called on the Marek home and accused Martha of poisoning his mother. Cool as ever, Martha called the police and laid a charge of trespass. Herbert Kittenberger was led angrily away still sprouting accusations. He was later released and warned to stay away from Marek.

One might think that this close call would have shaken Martha Marek up. Instead, the brazen murderess was emboldened by her narrow escape and began plotting her next caper. This involved, not a murder, but an oft-worked insurance scam. Martha had inherited a number of valuable paintings and tapestries from her aunt's estate. Many of these pieces she'd already sold off, but she now decided to cash in again. The valuables had been previously insured for $2,200. In October 1936, she phoned the police and reported a theft.

The detective sent to investigate the robbery was Rudolph Peternell, a fairly junior officer in the Vienna police force. Peternell was immediately suspicious of Marek's demeanor. She walked awkwardly, dragging her right leg and with her right arm dangling lifelessly by her side. Asked about her condition, Marek said that she had recently suffered a stroke. This surprised Peternell greatly. Martha Marek sometimes supplemented her income by performing as a cabaret singer and he'd just that morning read a newspaper article on a performance she'd given. She'd looked well enough in the accompanying picture.

His suspicions thus aroused, Inspector Peternell began looking into Marek's background. He learned that she had been born in Sopron, Hungary 38 years earlier and had been adopted at an early age. Her adoptive father, Rudolph Lowenstein, had later abandoned the family and Martha had been sent to a charitable institution in Vienna. At age 12, she'd been returned to her adoptive mother and had begun working as an errand girl in a dress shop.

Slim and dark-haired, Martha was a very pretty girl and in 1911, when she was 13, she caught the eye of a wealthy department store owner named Moritz Fritsch. With the approval of Martha's mother, she became his ward, moving into his luxurious villa in fashionable Moedling. Fritsch pampered Martha and paid for a top class education that included finishing schools in England and France. In exchange, the teenaged Martha became her 62-year-old patron's lover. When Fritsch died in August 1923, he left the bulk of his estate to her.

Three months after Fritsch's death, the newly wealthy Martha met and married Emil Marek, then an engineering student at the Vienna Technical Institute. And here things really got interesting for Inspector Peternell. He learned how Martha and her new husband had squandered Moritz Fritsch's fortune on a succession of grandiose, but ultimately unsuccessful schemes; he learned about Emil Marek's crudely amputated leg and the subsequent court case; he learned of the four suspicious deaths linked to Martha Marek.

In the meantime, another line of inquiry had also borne fruit. Peternell was able to track down the dealers who had bought items from Marek, items that she was now claiming as stolen. Marek soon found herself under arrest and charged with fraud.

But that was the least of her problems. The bodies of Emil Marek, Ingeborg Marek, Suzanne Lowenstein and Felicitas Kittenberger had been exhumed and found to contain large quantities of thallium, commonly in use as rat poison at the time. Marek had been found to be a frequent purchaser of the poison, based on the registers kept by local pharmacists.

Martha Marek when on trial for four counts of murder on May 2, 1938, drawing large crowds to the Vienna courthouse. Those who were lucky enough to get a seat in the courtroom were treated to a number of feisty exchanges between Martha (dubbed the "Devil in Petticoats," by the media) and the State's Attorney. Marek was warned that she faced a death sentence if found guilty and urged to confess in exchange for a lighter sentence. She stoutly refused.

In the end, that was to prove a foolhardy decision. The case against her was overwhelming, with over 100 witnesses called for the prosecution. It was no surprise when she was eventually found guilty and sentenced to death.

The execution of Martha Marek caused somewhat of a moral quandary in Austria. No woman had been executed in the country for over 60 years and many expected Marek's sentence to be commuted. Austria, however, had recently been incorporated into Germany by Hitler's Anschluss, and the death penalty had been returned to the statute books.

And so it was that, on December 6, 1938, Martha Marek was led onto the scaffold before the newly erected guillotine. In the days leading up to her execution, Martha had claimed paralysis. She'd had to be pushed around in a wheelchair. Now, though, there was no sign of her affliction. She wrestled with the guards and managed to land a kick on executioner Johann Reichhart before she was subdued and forced to kneel. Then the blade fell and neatly removed her head.

Body Parts

It was the body parts – found floating in the water off Clifford Pier – that first alerted the Singapore Police to the possibility of a serial killer. The corpse had been wrapped in black plastic bags, sectioned in such a way as to suggest that this was no ordinary murder. The killer quite obviously possessed some skill with a knife – a surgeon perhaps, or maybe a butcher. The police were still pondering that question when a second bag of human remains washed up on March 16, 1995.

By now authorities had a lead on the probable victim. He was a South African tourist by the name of Gerard Lowe, recently arrived in Singapore on a shopping junket. Lowe had been checked in at the River View Hotel, where he was sharing a room with another man, a Brit named Simon Davis. Davis, however, had since checked out and had apparently boarded a plane to Thailand. At least that was what immigration records said. A bit of delving quickly revealed that Simon Davis was actually serving a prison term in Britain. The man using his passport was John Martin Scripps, a globetrotting psychopath who the British media would dub, "The Tourist from Hell."

John Martin Scripps was born in Letchworth, Hertfordshire on December 9, 1959. Like many fledgling serial killers, he had difficulties in childhood. His much-loved father, Leonard, committed suicide when John was just nine, leaving the boy devastated. Thereafter, he developed learning disabilities and was eventually diagnosed with dyslexia.

At age 14, Scripps disappeared in France while on a cadet training trip. He remained at large for several weeks, supporting himself by petty crime. Eventually caught, he was returned to Britain. A year later, he appeared in juvenile court charged with burglary. Thereafter, he dropped out of school. Unable to read or write and therefore virtually unemployable, Scripps turned to the only way he knew to earn a living, a life of crime.

Scripps racked up his first adult conviction in 1978, when he was found guilty of indecent assault and given a fine of £40. Shortly afterwards, he traveled to Israel to work on a kibbutz. That brief sojourn ended in a robbery conviction and jail time.

In 1979, Scripps was in Canada when he met Maria Pilar Arellanos, a 17-year-old Mexican national. The couple married in London a year later and settled down to a life together. But that life was soon disrupted when Scripps was arrested for burglary in 1982. Maria stood by her man until 1985, when Scripps absconded from his sentence while on home leave. Then she divorced him and married a police officer, something that reportedly sent Scripps into a rage. There wasn't much he could do about it, though. A wanted fugitive, he fled the UK and embarked on a sojourn to South America and South-East Asia. There, he began working for a drug syndicate, smuggling narcotics into Europe, using various aliases.

Scripps new career as a drug mule came to a premature end when he was arrested at Heathrow airport in 1987. Tried and found guilty of drug trafficking offenses, he was sentenced to seven years in prison, with six more years added in 1992, after yet another escape attempt. Scripps, however, put his time behind bars to good use. He trained as a butcher, a skill he'd soon apply to a gruesome purpose.

John Martin Scripps had proved himself to be a significant flight risk, having absconded from three prior home leave furlongs. Yet the British prison system was prepared to give him another chance. In August 1993, he was transferred from the high-security Albany Prison to the medium-security Mount Prison in Hemel Hempstead. A year later, while on a period of home leave, Scripps again flew the coop. He embarked again on one of his global adventures. This one would have tragic consequences for at least four innocent people.

Having made his way out of the UK, Scripps traveled through the Netherlands, Belgium, and France in order to throw the authorities off his trail. Eventually, he ended up in Spain, and from there he boarded a flight to Mexico. Maria had in the interim divorced her second husband, and Scripps was determined to win back her heart. Maria, who would later describe the slick-talking psychopath as, "the sweetest man I have ever known," was easily convinced. Before long they had moved together into an apartment in Mexico City.

But Scripps' globetrotting ways were far from over. In December 1994, he traveled to Singapore, Bangkok, and Hong Kong and also visited the United States, where he set up bank accounts in San Diego and San Francisco. In January 1995, he was in Belize, when 28-year-old British national Timothy McDowell went missing. A total of £21,000 was subsequently transferred from McDowell's account to the US bank accounts Scripps had set up. When Scotland Yard detectives arrived in Mexico to follow up leads in the case, Scripps fled again, heading back to Asia.

Scripps had by now developed a deadly efficient M.O. At Singapore Airport, he struck up a conversation with fellow traveler Gerard Lowe. Scripps, like all psychopaths, was amiable and charming. First, he sold Lowe on his credentials as someone who knew Singapore well. Then he convinced him that they could save a considerable amount of money by sharing a hotel room. Lowe, a first-time visitor to Singapore, was only too happy to have met someone with local knowledge. Little did he know that his newfound friend was carrying in his luggage a murder kit, containing a stun gun, a builder's hammer, several butcher's knives and a number of pairs of handcuffs. They'd barely checked into the room when Scripps incapacitated Lowe with the stun gun and beat him to death with the hammer.

Over the next three days, Scripps continued to live in the hotel room. During that time, he dissected Lowe's body in the bathtub, cutting it into ten pieces (this would become a trademark of Scripps' method). The body parts were placed in black garbage bags and crammed into suitcases. Scripps was picked up on surveillance cameras on a number of occasions lugging these suitcases out of the hotel. He also visited reception to inform hotel staff that he was now staying in the room alone, having thrown Lowe out over an alleged homosexual advance.

Gerard Lowe's mutilated remains would surface in Singapore harbor within days of Scripps disposing of them. By then, the killer was on the move again, traveling to Thailand. On the flight, he was seated next to Canadian tourists Sheila Damude, 47, and her 23-year-old son Darin. Turning on the charm, Scripps was soon regaling his fellow travelers with tales of Phuket, where they were bound. After they disembarked, he convinced them to share a taxi. He checked into a room adjacent to theirs at the resort. That was on March 15. The following day, Scripps checked out of the hotel and informed the receptionist that he would also be settling the Damude's bill. Sheila and Darren Damude's dismembered bodies would later be found in a disused tin mine, about five miles from the hotel. Each had been cut into ten pieces and their skulls bore fractures that had been caused by a builder's hammer.

On March 19, Scripps flew back into Singapore, oblivious to the fact that Gerard Lowe's remains had been found. He was arrested at the airport and a search of his luggage turned up documents and credit cards belonging to the Damudes and to Gerrard Lowe, as well as his murder kit. Charged with murder, he was taken to Changi Prison where he readily admitted killing Lowe. However, in Scripps version of events, the murder had been unpremeditated. According to Scripps, he had struck Lowe after the latter made a homosexual advance. He'd then panicked and fled, contacting a British acquaintance to dispose of the body. Asked for his accomplice's name he refused to give it, saying the man was an underworld figure who might harm his family.

Scripps was still telling that story when he went on trial for murder on October 2, 1995. The Singapore justice system does not employ juries and it would be Judge T.S. Sinnathuray who would weigh the evidence and decide on the verdict and sentence. On November 7, Judge Sinnathuray adjourned the trial for three days in order to consider his verdict. He returned on November 10 and after presenting a succinct review of the evidence, delivered the verdict most had been expecting.

"Altogether, the factual evidence reinforces the decision I have made, for it puts beyond doubt that Scripps is guilty on the charge of murder.

"The sentence of this court upon you is that you will be taken from this place to a lawful prison and taken to a place to be hanged by the neck until you are dead. And may the Lord have mercy on your soul."

John Martin Scripps, who had up until that point been laughing and joking with his guards, appeared visibly shocked by the outcome.

Scripps' attorneys initially stated that they would appeal the sentence. However, on January 4, 1996, four days before they were due to be heard, Scripps suddenly announced that he had accepted his fate and would not be appealing, nor petitioning the president for clemency.

While he awaited execution, details emerged of at least two more murders in which he was implicated. Accountant William Shackel disappeared while holidaying in Cancún, Mexico. He'd last been seen in the company of a man matching Scripps description and $6,000 of his travelers' checks had been cashed on the day he went missing. Tom Wenger, a homosexual prostitute, was killed in San Francisco on March 28, 1994. His body was found in a dumpster, cut up into Scripps' trademark ten pieces. Witnesses asked to identify the man they'd seen with Wenger, readily picked Scripps from a photo array.

Scripps, of course, would never stand trial for those murders. He went to the gallows in Singapore on April 19, 1996.

The Brighton Trunk Murders

The city of Brighton has long been a popular seaside resort and tourist destination, particularly for day-trippers from London. Situated in East Sussex on the English south coast, it boasts many attractions, including the Brighton Palace Pier, the Royal Pavilion and the opulent, Victorian era, Grand Hotel. Over eight million visitors are drawn here annually, attracted by its offbeat shopping areas, vibrant nightlife and thriving arts and music scenes.

But like any large city, Brighton has its dark side. In October 1984, the Provisional Irish Republican Army (IRA) detonated a bomb at the Grand Hotel in an effort to assassinate Prime Minister Margaret Thatcher. Thatcher survived, but five others did not. The city also saw scenes of mass rioting during the mid-1960s when rival teenaged gangs of "Mods" and "Rockers" fought out brutal battles on the streets.

Brighton, of course, has also seen its fair share of murders. And bizarrely enough, three of the most high-profile cases all involved bodies left in trunks. The first of those occurred in 1831, when a man named John Holloway murdered his wife, packed her body in a trunk and transported her by wheelbarrow to Preston Park, where he buried her. Holloway was soon arrested for the crime and was later tried, found guilty and hanged at Lewes.

The other two cases both occurred in 1934, and although unrelated, the investigation into the first murder led fortuitously to the discovery of the second.

June 17, 1934, was Derby day in England and the Brighton railway station was teeming with commuters heading to Epsom Downs for the famous horse race. It is, therefore, unsurprising that when one of those commuters checked a black plywood trunk into the luggage office, the staff paid little attention to the man. Eleven days later the trunk was still there – and it was beginning to smell.

When luggage clerk William Vinnicombe went to inspect the box, he noticed a dark substance leaking from it. He decided immediately to call in the police.

Chief Inspector Ronald Donaldson supervised the opening of the trunk. It contained the dismembered torso of a young woman, deemed to be between 21 and 28 years old, and five months pregnant at the time of her death. A bulletin to other rail stations soon turned up the woman's legs, stuffed into a suitcase that had been left at London's King's Cross. The head and arms, however, were never found making it impossible for the police to make an identification.

There was one suspect, though. The police speculated that the woman might have died as the result of a botched abortion, and they soon honed in on a reputed backstreet abortionist, Dr. Edward Massiah. Brought in for questioning, Massiah denied involvement and also hinted that he had a long list of prominent clients whose names he was prepared to leak to the press if the police continued to "harass him." Facing pressure from above, Chief Inspector Donaldson was forced to let the matter drop.

With that avenue of investigation closed, the police tried a new approach. First, they compiled a list of women who had recently been reported missing in Brighton and the surrounding areas, turning up forty names. Then they began calling on the friends and families of those women, trying to establish whether the body in the trunk might be one of the missing.

One of those who made the list was Violette Kaye, a still attractive 44-year-old who had once been a professional dancer. These days, however, Kaye was reputed to finance her alcohol and morphine habits by working as a prostitute. That is, at least, until she'd suddenly disappeared on May 10, 1934.

Kaye's live-in lover was a small-time crook named Tony Mancini. When the police called on him in mid-July, Mancini was the model of co-operation. Violette had left him after a quarrel, he said. As far as he knew, she was living and working in France.

The police had no reason to doubt Mancini's story. In truth, Violette Kaye had never been that high up on their list of prospects. At 44 years old she was too old to be the body in the trunk. But there were one or two points in Mancini's statement that the police wanted to clarify.

On July 15, two officers called on Mancini's lodgings for a second interview. His landlady told them that he was out, but invited them to wait in his room. Immediately on entering the premises, the officers noticed an unpleasant smell. It appeared to be coming from a large trunk, standing in the center of the room. Prying the lid from the trunk, the officers discovered its source - the decayed body of Violette Kay, over two months dead.

A search was immediately launched for Tony Mancini, and the police soon discovered that Mancini had boarded a train to London that very morning. Yet even as telegrams were being dispatched to various jurisdictions warning them to be on the lookout, Mancini was alighting from the train in Maidstone, Kent, having decided that it was too risky to travel to the capital. He was arrested later that day walking along a road just outside of town. Initially, he identified himself as Jack Notyre. Then, in an apparent change of heart, he admitted that he was the man they were looking for. "But I didn't murder her," he assured the officers.

Mancini was taken to Maidstone police station, where it was discovered that neither Tony Mancini, nor Jack Notyre, was his real name. His name was, in fact, Cecil England. He was also not the East End tough he tried to portray himself as, but from a well-off, middle-class family. His father worked as a civil servant in Whitehall.

Mancini, however, had been drawn to criminality from an early age. After deserting from the RAF, he'd hooked up with notorious East End gangster, 'Harry Boy' Sabini. Mancini had become an enforcer in Sabini's gang and had quickly developed a reputation for brutality. It was rumored that he'd once hacked off a man's hand with a cleaver, and had put another man's hand through a meat grinder.

Then, in 1932, Mancini met Violette Kaye, a down-on-her-luck former showgirl just getting started in the dangerous world of prostitution. Violette needed a pimp and protector and Mancini offered his services. Despite their age different (Violette was 17 years older than Tony) they were soon lovers.

In 1934, the pair decided to move to Brighton. Still a beauty, with a slim and supple body from her dancing days, Violette had by then built up a roster of well-to-do clients, many of whom would drive all the way from London to spend a few hours with her. She was earning good money, even if a sizeable portion of it went to feed her addictions.

But Mancini soon tired of being a kept man. Seeking some independence, he got himself a job as a cook and waiter at the Skylark Café.

Five days after Mancini started his new job, on Thursday, May 10, 1934, Violette showed up at the Skylark somewhat the worse for drink. She appeared agitated and Mancini tried to calm her down by seating her at a table and offering to cook her a meal. However, when he stopped to exchange a few words with a pretty young waitress on his way to the kitchen, Violette exploded. She began shouting, accusing Mancini of having an affair. Then she burst into tears and fled the restaurant. The damage had been done, however. Mancini's boss told him to hand in his apron.

According to the story Mancini now told the police, he was angry with Violette for the trouble she'd caused. However, by the time he got home later that evening he had calmed down. He still loved her, and the loss of his meager wages was hardly going to put him in the poorhouse. He entered the darkened apartment fully prepared to forgive her.

Violette was asleep on the bed when he entered, but she was so still that Mancini was concerned. He walked over to gently shake her awake and it was then that he saw the blood and realized that she was dead. He immediately assumed that one of her clients must have murdered her and his first instinct was to call the police. But he quickly disregarded that idea. He was an ex-con, with motive and opportunity. It didn't take a genius to work out that the finger of blame would be directed at him. And if found guilty of murder, he was likely to end up on the end of a rope.

Panicked, Mancini decided to hide the body, at least until he figured out what to do. The large trunk sitting in the corner of the room seemed perfect, so he stuffed Violette's body inside. Then he got to work concocting his cover story. Violette's sister-in-law was due to visit in a few days, so the first order of business was to forestall her. A telegram, purportedly from Violette, saying that she had moved to France, did the trick.

Over the days that followed, Mancini moved to a new apartment, getting a friend to help him lug the heavy trunk. He had stayed there for over two months, with Violette's corpse rotting in the case just feet away from where he slept. It was only once the police came asking questions that he had panicked and run.

Mancini's story sounded incredibly farfetched and the police weren't buying it. Charged with murder, he was remanded to appear in the Lewes Crown Court in December 1934.

It looked like an open and shut case. The prosecution had evidence of an argument, witnesses who claimed Mancini had boasted about the murder, a partially burned coal hammer that might have been the murder weapon, blood on Mancini's clothing, the deceptive telegram sent to Violette's sister-in-law, Mancini's concealment of the body and the lies he'd told about Violette's whereabouts. It looked to all the world like Tony Mancini was going to the gallows. The newspapers certainly thought so and had already pronounced as much.

But they reckoned without one important factor, Mancini's barrister, Norman Birkett KC. A quite brilliant lawyer, Birkett was known for his mild, friendly persona. Always calm, always respectful, Birkett never lost his cool, never harangued a witness. This demeanor was said to have won many a jury over to his side.

Birkett's strategy was simple, to cast doubt on every piece of evidence presented by the prosecution. He achieved this with admirable precision. Witnesses were presented to testify that Mancini and Violette never quarreled and appeared devoted to each other. The witnesses who claimed that Mancini had boasted about the murder were made to contradict one another. The blood on Mancini's clothing was proven to have got there weeks after Violette's death. The coal hammer found in the apartment could not be proven to have been there at the time of the murder. The autopsy report proved to be less than conclusive. Birkett even got the famed pathologist, Sir Bernard Spilsbury, to admit on the stand that Violette might have died of a drug overdose. It all added up to reasonable doubt – and lots of it.

One bothersome issue still remained for Birkett to resolve. If Mancini was innocent why hadn't he called the police? Why had he hidden the body? To address this issue, Birkett called Mancini himself to the stand. And Mancini's response to Birkett's question could not have been better answered if it had been deliberately scripted. "What me?" he said incredulously when asked why he hadn't called the police. The implication was obvious. How was an ex-con going to get a fair shake in circumstances like this?

In the end, it took the jury just over two hours to deliver a "Not guilty" verdict. Given Birkett's brilliant defense, it was the only verdict they could have presented – except that it was the wrong one. That much would become evident over forty years later.

On November 28, 1976, the News of the World ran a story under the banner "I've Got Away With Murder." In it, Tony Mancini told a different version of events to that presented at his trial. He still wasn't admitting to willful murder, but he was accepting responsibility for Violette's death.

According to Mancini's new account, he and Violette had argued at the Skylark Café and had continued their argument when he returned home later that evening. During the course of that quarrel, Violette had complained of being cold, and Mancini had crouched down to light a fire in the grate. While he was doing so, Violette had picked up the coal hammer and struck him a glancing blow. Mancini jumped up and snatched the hammer away from her. He started walking away, but Violette screamed after him, "Give me that hammer!" Instinctively, he turned and tossed it, striking her on the head. Violette collapsed immediately to the floor.

Mancini's ire was up now. Crouching over Violette he began shaking her, then slamming her head against the floor. "Look what you've made me do!" he shouted as he continued his assault. It was only when blood started flowing from her mouth that he realized he was not slamming her head to the carpeted floor, as he'd thought, but against the metal fire grate.

"I honestly didn't mean to kill her," Mancini asserted in the newspaper article. "I just lost control in the heat of the moment."

Tony Mancini could, of course, not be retried, meaning that he literally got away with murder. As for the other Brighton trunk murder, it remains unsolved to this day.

For more True Crime books by Robert Keller please visit

http://bit.ly/kellerbooks

Printed in Poland
by Amazon Fulfillment
Poland Sp. z o.o., Wrocław